Look What You Made Me Do

Confronting Heartbreak & Harassment in Big Law

Erin Gordon

D1603655

Novels By Erin Gordon

Cheer
Heads or Tails
Beshert
Peeps

For C, A & E

"If guys don't want me to write bad songs about them,
then they shouldn't do bad things."
— Taylor Swift

This is a true story.

Descriptions of my years in Big Law are accurate to the best of my recollection. Because human memory is imperfect and because I was not a neutral observer to the events, I supplemented and verified my memories with current interviews as well as documents — including memos, emails and handwritten logs — from the time in question. Any dialogue in the narrative — as opposed to the interview section — has been recreated to represent the essence of my recollections and should not be taken as word-for-word transcripts.

Names of all key players — including colleagues and the name of the law firm at the center of this story — have been changed. There are no invented or "composite" characters.

August 7, 1991

Memorandum to Marty Martinez

Re: Erin Gordon

I've just received a memorandum from Erin Gordon on a contract interpretation issue in the Mallner case that is the best piece of work I've received from a summer clerk in years. It is very well-written, crisply analyzed, well organized, error-free, and shows fine attention to detail. I would expect to see this level of quality from a senior associate. Coming from a summer clerk, it is a nice surprise.

Jon B. Streeter*

* Jon B. Streeter was a partner at Orrick, Herrington & Sutcliffe when he wrote this memo (on which I was cc'd) to Martinez, the head of Orrick's summer associate program. In 2014, Streeter was appointed to the California Court of Appeal, First District, Division 4.

July 23, 1994

To: Frederick Duncan

From: Jasper Brook

...Ms. Gordon is the least productive associate in the litigation group. The response to her work has been mixed, at best. I suspect that she will become, if not already, a problem associate....The one memo she prepared for me was mediocre, and displayed weak analytical skills and no depth whatsoever....From all indications she is an attorney who is about to be identified as one who is not going to make it.

Prologue
Late July 1994

Trembling and sweating, I knocked on the door of managing partner Frederick Duncan's office. I took a seat on his guest couch. Eleven days before, I'd turned 26. Frederick was in his mid-50's, the same age as my father. He regarded me — a lowly first-year associate — stone-faced from behind his desk. I glanced down at the meticulously prepared notes on my legal pad, took a breath and began to speak.

"In the nine months I've worked at Schiffer Mulligan, I've been subjected to threats to 'ruin my career' and other unfair treatment to which I put the firm on notice by speaking to a partner numerous times. It continued nonetheless. I've seen the memo Jasper Brook wrote to you. I object to being termed a 'problem' associate...."

Despite Duncan's prodding, I refused to reveal the name of the staff person who had seen Brook's inappropriate and nasty memo on a shared printer, quickly made a copy, and secretly brought it to me, risking her job to do so. Instead, I continued on from my notes, delineating unrelenting examples of slights, belittling, and rumors, culminating in the sickening Brook memo, which — in its entirety — made shocking references to my romantic and sex life.

The moment I uttered the phrase "hostile work environment," a legal term related to sexual harassment, Frederick's demeanor transformed. Within nanoseconds, he grabbed a pen and wrote down my every next word on his own legal pad, his spine elongated as he leaned stiffly forward. His expressionless eyes remained trained on mine.

Despite my conviction, the truth of my words, my hands and legs shook. And within just a few sentences, my voice cracked and I began to cry. Like most women who cry in professional settings, I began apologizing profusely, diluting the power of my words.

I hated myself in that moment.

It was no victory lap.

I felt vulnerable, infantilized.

I was frightened and so, so frustrated.

I never wanted it to get to this point.

But I'd been pushed to the brink. I was left with no alternative. After nine awful months, the Jasper Brook memo forced me to finally put it all on the line, to raise with the law office's most powerful partner the litany of wrongs I'd endured.

What would happen to my career now?

Chapter One

2023

As a brand-new attorney at Schiffer Mulligan, the firm I joined after graduating from law school, I experienced insidious, degrading treatment by other lawyers at the firm. I was just 25, in the earliest days of my first professional job.

We all know about the Harvey Weinsteins, the awful #metoo stories of overt sexual harassment.

I was not groped or propositioned.

What I experienced was repeated micro-harassments so subtle as to be plausibly denied. Yet I was emotionally shredded by these actions. Within the first weeks at the firm, my identity and self-worth were eviscerated. The events caused me to adopt a view of myself that I'm discovering only now was empirically wrong.

What I experienced in Big Law is harder to see than the typical #metoo scenario, but it's real and pervasive. It's harder to pinpoint with a hashtag (#subtleundermining?) but it's abusive and dangerous nonetheless. It's likely happened to you, your daughter, your sister, your wife, your friend. One of my (male) friends who read a draft of this manuscript emailed me: "What you experienced is so brutal and amplified by the fact that I fear it is not atypical." And men, you've likely observed this going on in your own workplace or even contributed to it without realizing the impact.

What happened at Schiffer Mulligan derailed my whole career, and several experts I interviewed confirmed that treatment like this still happens in Big Law today. Unlike Hollywood or other industries, the legal profession has not yet had a moral reckoning, its #metoo comeuppance.

It's too late to scrape together the career I should have had. But if nothing else, my story can shine a light on persistent gender-based discrimination, inequality and abuse in our culture. It also may inspire others to examine whether their own long-held shame — in whatever context — is actually misplaced.

I worked in Big Law long before hashtags and social media movements. Yet there's no statute of limitations on truth. It's not too late to share my story of heartbreak, of harassment and, ultimately, of reclaiming identity and self-esteem. I hope this story will inspire others, especially women, to reconsider past trauma, to critically re-think the negative stories we tell ourselves, to reclaim our own narratives so that we let go of the shame, the responsibility we might have wrongfully placed on ourselves. By rejecting abusers' and gaslighters' false version of events, we can finally step into our power.

***

I decided to tell the story of my first year in Big Law shortly after a summer evening in 2022 that I spent in Lake Tahoe with the family we've been vacationing with for three generations. The dinner was winding down. The burritos had been consumed. Only tortilla chip fragments remained, none large enough to even scrape the bottom of the queso bowl. Ice cream drumsticks had been passed out to the dozen close family friends lounging on the patio. Gnats and bats emerged in the dusk, the rumble of trucks on the nearby road calmed.

"Can I talk to you for a second?" Kelli asked, beckoning me inside.

"Sure," I said, baffled as to what she wanted to discuss that required our separation from everyone else. After all, our two families had been like one ever since our dads met in college in the 1950's.

Kelli led me into a back bedroom of the VRBO her family had rented for the week. She closed the door. "I'm kind of nervous," she said.

What in the world? I thought. Kelli is hilarious, open, self-assured, and like a little sister to me. I'd never seen her like this.

Had I said something inappropriate during our week together?

Was she mad at me?

Had her breast cancer returned?

"So," she began, "I've been wanting to tell you something this week but the time never seemed right." She took a deep inhale. "When I was in high school," she continued, taking the conversation in a direction I absolutely was not expecting, "I had what I now know was an inappropriate relationship with a teacher."

Blood rose to my brain, circulating loudly in my ears.

Kelli went on to tell me that beginning in the 9th grade, she'd been groomed for years by a 40-something married teacher at her high school, who had also been her academic advisor. She was 14 then and believed with all her heart that she was in love with him and he with her. Within a couple of years, *before* she turned 18 (the age of consent in California), they were sleeping together, and the relationship continued through her first year in college. "It was consensual," Kelli said.

"Hold up!" I stopped her for the first time. "Monica Lewinsky initially insisted that her relationship with Bill Clinton had been consensual. But now, as a mature woman, she grasps the warped power dynamic at play and —"

"Yup, yup, I get it. I'm realizing a lot of things now," Kelli said. "Like, for so long, I had all this shame, all this guilt that I'd had a long-term relationship with a married man. It resulted in OCD, eating issues, other problems."

I slumped back in the wicker chair. As awful as I felt learning that Kelli had been abused as an adolescent by a man nearly three times her age, I felt far worse — sickened, actually — that she'd lived for decades ashamed, certain that *she'd* been to blame.

Kelli continued her story. Many teachers and administrators at her high school had known of the inappropriate relationship but not one adult stepped in to protect her. Kelli brought this up to me now because she was considering a lawsuit against the high school using California's temporary extension of the five-year statute of limitations for childhood abuse, and her name might soon be in the media.

A heavy pall cast over my body. As I absorbed the severity of her words, my body running hot from blood coursing through my torso and limbs, my gut swirling uncomfortably, I also felt a distinct switch flip in my brain.

At nearly 50, Kelli was dissecting that long-held narrative and reclaiming the power and agency that had been snatched from her by a disturbed older man. She excavated and re-read her teenage journals chronicling the details of the relationship, which she now understood was unequivocal childhood sexual abuse. She was finally — but also suddenly — seeing herself and a formative experience in a wholly new way. She now grasped that what really happened was that she'd been preyed upon, that she'd done nothing but behave exactly how most girls going through puberty would have when receiving special attention from a beloved teacher. Now, in considering filing a lawsuit, she wanted not money but for the school to launch a formal, public investigation so other women who may also have been victims could come forward before the extended statute of limitations lapsed at the end of 2022.

Kelli's bravery in facing painful actions at the hands of adults — both the abuser himself and, as importantly, the bystanders who failed to protect her — triggered a powerful shift in me. Instantly and profoundly.

Could I, too, reexamine a story I'd been telling myself *for decades?*

Like Kelli, I held deep shame — for me, about my first year in law. Aside from the months I had a dangerously sick newborn, it was unequivocally the worst, saddest year of my life. If Kelli's high school journals reflected not, as she'd expected, gleeful complicity in an affair, but rather the psychological effects of being groomed by a predator, maybe my own behavior that first year I worked as a lawyer wasn't actually embarrassing or pathetic at all. Maybe I might discover that I, too, had been on the wrong end of something sinister.

I launched my legal career long before widespread understanding of the psychological harms of victim-blaming and gaslighting, both interpersonal tools employed by powerful people — like lawyers — precisely to keep vulnerable individuals down. Now, though, I could apply those new-to-me concepts to past events.

Years after her "relationship" with President Clinton, Monica Lewinsky published in *Vanity Fair* a powerful article, "Emerging from 'The House of Gaslight' in the Age of #metoo." She wrote, "I've lived for such a long time in the House of Gaslight, clinging to my experiences as they unfolded in my 20s and railing against the untruths that painted me as an unstable stalker and Servicer in Chief. An inability to deviate from the internal script of what I actually experienced left little room for re-evaluation; I cleaved to what I 'knew.'...What it means to confront a long-held belief (one clung to like a life raft in the middle of the ocean) is to challenge your own perceptions and allow the *pentimento* painting that is hidden beneath the surface to emerge and be seen in the light of a new day."

Like Kelli, like Lewinsky, I spent decades terrified to take a close look at my first year as a young female attorney at a San Francisco law firm. These negative feelings toward myself reveal my own complicity in gender stereotyping, in accepting the gaslighters' interpretation of events.

The years at my second firm, which I joined just 12 months into my career, were not much better. Two firms, two terrible results? I could only conclude that *I* was the problem. That was my default explanation.

Thanks to Kelli's bravery, I now understand that one result *triggered* the other: the "failure" at the first firm left me little chance of success at the second. And neither was the result of my capacity or potential as a lawyer. It was akin to what economists call a "doom loop," where one negative event sets off another.

Kelli's revelation inspired me to dive deep and reconsider whether my own decades-old shame was perhaps similarly misplaced. The only way for me to do that was by writing.

Soon after becoming a mom, I wrote a novel about how vulnerable it is to be a parent. A few years later, as I observed my relationships with old friends shifting, I wrote a novel exploring the bounds of loyalty. Then, when I was trying to reconcile my atheist beliefs with my strong identity as a Jew, I wrote a novel about love and faith. In my early '50's, I wrote a journey story in the vein of *The Wizard of Oz* and Cheryl Strayed's *Wild* about a middle-aged woman who embarks on an epic road trip in an effort to find her place in the world. In other words, I process what I'm personally grappling with through writing.

As a high school senior in 1986, I took the AP History exam. Designed to evaluate a student's ability to sort through facts and opinions, it was and still is structured as a document-based question. That was my first exposure to the concept of primary sources: correspondence, legislative history, interviews and meeting minutes. I also learned that secondary sources — including analyses, commentaries and interpretive texts — can add value to a primary source.

I was not a strong history student but sorting deliberately un-chronological primary and secondary sources, mixed up with irrelevant materials, puzzling out what to discard, evaluating sources' credibility, and devising a reasoned conclusion about what actually happened...those were tasks I enjoyed and excelled at. Making sense of things, assigning everything to categories and then writing about them, soothes me. It makes me feel safe in the world.

But to write about my experiences in Big Law, I would have to take a look at some primary sources. I'd have to revisit "The File."

***

My old Ikea desk houses a drawer of hanging files with folders labeled things like "Kids' Report Cards," "State Bar," and "Stanford." Once or twice a year, I turn on a podcast and clean out the old receipts and no-longer-necessary paperwork. If I don't, the overstuffed files make it challenging to close the drawer. However, despite my diligent culling, there's one file that, once shut, I never, ever opened to read or remove anything from: "Schiffer Mulligan." Once I slid the very last item in "The File" in the fall of 1994 when I left the firm, I didn't re-open it until December 2022, shortly after I began working on this story.

My home office has a split personality. On my husband's side, huge stacks of papers — complex legal agreements, bills from 20 years ago, old Post-It Notes that have lost their stickiness — mingle with cords to unknown devices and mugs with cold tea bags. My sentimental husband still uses the roll-top desk he got for his bar mitzvah. My modern desk, in contrast, is crisp and orderly, with files clearly labeled, legal pads lined up edge to edge. This office is a metaphor, a reflection of our relationship to the past. My husband has a tough time letting "stuff" go, keeping it out of nostalgia or an aversion to facing painful memories. I, on the other hand, ascribe to the "outer order contributes to inner calm" philosophy. Yet I, too, have an aversion to facing painful memories, which makes the fact that I *kept* The File — amidst 30 years of twice-yearly drawer cleaning — incredibly notable and puzzling. Some friends have suggested it was brave to keep it. But I'm inclined to say it was the opposite — I was scared to even touch The File, to face the primary sources it might contain.

I didn't remember precisely what was in The File, which measured more than an inch thick, but I long feared that it contained items I'd find embarrassing or absurdly painful. I *thought* I'd find emails proving I'd been pathetic and weak. I *thought* I'd find evidence of me begging to be taken back by a man I now find repulsive. I *thought* I'd find emails written to law partners that were unprofessional. And yet I'd kept The File. Why hadn't I just dumped it to help me forget about that awful year altogether?

I always tell my Gen Z children that anything they put online can be screenshot by anyone and brought up at a later date. The File turned out to be the analog version of that. When I finally did re-open it, I discovered a treasure trove of primary sources like I learned about in AP History; specifically, memos and emails written by me and others. The File is so old that some pages had rust marks from the paperclips holding them together. Rubber bands around other stacks disintegrated in my hands.

Because memory is messy, The File was invaluable in filling in my incomplete and forgotten recollections. The words in it unequivocally told a different story than what I'd long feared. I'm now unafraid, as kids these days say, to "show the receipts." I found not a single cringe-worthy item — no letters begging a man to stay or evidence that I'd embarrassed myself in front of powerful law firm partners. Importantly, that's not because

I'd thrown items like that out. If they weren't in The File, that meant they didn't exist because, again, I hadn't dared to even open The File for nearly 30 years.

It turns out that memos I'd written to management about what I was experiencing were articulate, unemotional and, I see with three decades of hindsight, surprisingly badass. The File showed that what I encountered during my sad, life-altering year at Schiffer Mulligan was inappropriate and some events so gratuitously mean they made me nauseous to re-live them.

***

When I first considered re-examining my painful time at Schiffer Mulligan, a project I knew would be labor-intensive and emotionally fraught, I had two conversations within days of each other that persuaded me to move forward. First, I told my long-time therapist (whom I've been seeing monthly since Emmy, my now 20-year-old daughter, was ill as a newborn) that my next writing project would be about a terrible year from my distant past.

I supplied a few more details. She nodded sagely. "Interesting timing."

"What do you mean?"

"Well," she said, as if it was the most obvious fact in the world, "you've been holding onto this story for thirty years. And now Emmy is in college and about to go out into the world."

As soon as I heard her say it, I realized she was exactly right, though it had not once occurred to me before then.

What would be the broad message, the cautionary tale for my daughter?

Don't become a lawyer?

Stand up for yourself?

Don't be fooled that sexism no longer exists in the workplace?

Would any advice I could have received in 1992 have prevented what happened later at Schiffer Mulligan?

Next, I told my husband about my plan to revisit how a relationship that turned sour led to my male colleagues and supervisors discussing my sex life and using erroneous facts about that relationship to make critical decisions about my career.

"You sure you want Emmy to read something like that?" he said.

I thought back to how weak and small, how confused and powerless I felt as a 25-year-old woman trying to make my way among a sea of powerful men. I didn't want it all to be in vain.

"Actually," I replied, "I think I'm writing it *for* Emmy."

The lesson of my story, I believe, is not so much what young women can do to prepare for the workplace. I now see that I did everything I could have — talked to partners I thought I could trust, spoke to management, even hired a lawyer — but nothing changed. In fact, it got worse.

No, the lesson is far more universal. Of course, we all make mistakes and we must 100 percent own up to our contributions to problems. But, for women in particular, often our worst feelings, our shame, our *vitriol* towards ourselves may actually be misplaced.

Writer Taffy Brodesser-Akner captured the need for this reassessment perfectly in her October 2023 *New York Times* story about the wild appeal of Taylor Swift concerts: "Eras [is actually] proof of concept, a woman looking back on her youth to remember what she is made of, not with shame but with curiosity and even delight. It had never occurred to me to look back on even my most carefree and innocuous eras with anything but shame."

Let's change that.

I want Emmy and other young adults to cultivate the self-awareness, the self-esteem that I didn't have, that — at 55 — I'm still seeking. As important, I want others who've blindly blamed themselves for old problems to reevaluate. Perhaps this singular story about life in Big Law — a microcosm of society at large — can inspire that.

***

I'm finally facing the profound grief (and newly understanding it as grief) that I long suppressed about my career, my income, my identity, about not living up to my potential. Deeply, deeply feminist, I've struggled for decades to reconcile that core element of my identity with the reality that I am completely supported by my husband, due in large part to my failure in law.

I spent 1993-1994 just barely able to get through each day and afterwards spent a long time recovering from that year, a year when I was certain I'd been my worst self. I had zero energy to analyze power structures, gender hierarchies, or the psychopathy of people I crossed paths with then. But 30 years later, I'm able to be self-reflective, to be raw, to make peace with my past mistakes, to speak my truth even if my voice shakes.

When I told a fellow writer friend what I was working on, she looked me in the eye, pointed to her forehead and said, "This was all at the very tip of your brain. It just needed a place to go."

I remembered then a fitness class I took in May of 2022 — two months *before* Kelli's revelation flipped that switch in my brain — when the instructor set up a station to slam a heavy medicine ball against a wall, catch it and slam it back again. I remembered that out of nowhere, with each violent slam, I began whispering the names of people in this story.

Jasper. Dixon. Ben. Tim. Mike. Malley. Fuck. You.

Even as I gained momentum, re-reading the old memos and emails that told a surprisingly different story from what I thought I'd remembered, I still feared that all those men — not to mention readers — will simply laugh. Or call me bitter. Or will berate me for being too weak to get over events from three decades ago.

Peeling back the proverbial bandage, I was stunned at how tender the old wound still was. I hadn't properly healed; I'd merely repressed the pain. More than once during my reporting and writing, I was tempted to abandon the project for fear of re-infecting that wound. As I read through The File, as I had video calls with a dozen former colleagues, I vacillated between determination and deep fear. My father, who once referred to that time in my life as "not your finest moment," pleaded, "Why don't you just forget about it?" But I'd done that for several decades, which only served to magnify my shame and further erode my self-esteem. Really, I reasoned, there seemed to be nowhere to go but up.

Kelli was an excellent model for me in moving from victim to creator. Maybe something therapeutic for me — and instructive or validating for others — could result from this work. Within weeks of that conversation with Kelli, I began reporting my own story using the skills I've honed for more than 25 years as a magazine and newspaper journalist specializing in legal affairs.

Chapter Two

2023

In the 1999 book *Walking Out on the Boys*, neurosurgeon Frances Conley — a female neurosurgeon and professor at Stanford Medical School — described the pervasive sexism and sexualized nature of her workplace in the early 1990's, the exact same period that I worked at Schiffer Mulligan. Conley briefly resigned from Stanford when one of the worst offenders was about to be named department chair, a resignation that sparked national headlines. She wrote, "So often women who bring a complaint of discrimination or sexual harassment become so emotional about events, their presentation is less than rational, in fact often is hysterical. Then, in domino fashion, the original abuse is followed by skepticism, followed by retribution for making a fuss in the first place, followed by termination or ostracism because people do not believe the 'mentally deranged' accuser."

Not only is this precisely what happened at Schiffer Mulligan, but it was what I feared would happen in writing a book about the experience, in being a late-blooming whistleblower.

Given the intensely personal nature of what happened, I did, of course, consider fictionalizing the experience, turning my own story into a novel. After all, I'd written several novels with themes that were personal to me.

But...

A male law firm partner specializing in employment law putting misogynistic thoughts about a female associate's private romantic life in a memo *in writing*?

Grown professionals drawing devil horns and a mustache on a young colleague's photo on display in a public space in the office?

The firm denying the woman's claims of a hostile work environment (despite written proof and a meticulous cataloging of events) but, at the same time, responding to those dismissed complaints with an immediate firm-wide change in policy to disadvantage future victims?

Readers would call that novel unbelievable.

I settled on a memoir format, but because I'm in no way impartial or neutral regarding the events at Schiffer Mulligan in 1993 and 1994, I took an extremely deliberate approach to this story. This is a memoir, but it's guided by generally accepted principles of journalism.

In the Stanford journalism program that I attended after (spoiler alert) I abandoned Big Law altogether, professors drilled into us the critical importance of accuracy, attribution, and balanced, fair and objective reporting. And these principles guided my journalism career.

But what happens when the reporter is also part of the story?

My approach was akin to Rebecca Skloot's in *The Immortal Life of Henrietta Lacks*, one of my all-time favorite books. In Skloot's case, she set out to research Henrietta Lacks, a long-forgotten woman who had a profound and unwitting impact on medicine and bioethics. After growing close to Lacks's family through years of interviews, Skloot became a part — a character, if you will — in Lacks's story.

Like *The Immortal Life of Henrietta Lacks,* this story is a mixture of journalism and memoir. I supported my own recollections with primary sources in The File as well as interviews in large part because of how my memory works. My husband can tell you all of the cars he's ever owned along with most of their license plate numbers. He knows off the top of his head the phone numbers for taxi services in cities he's never lived in.

But my mind works differently. I don't remember a single book we read in Mrs. Witte's sophomore English class. But I do remember the house dresses she wore to school, that she once used the term "Jewess" in front of me. I remember the time that, when referring to her male colleague whom I'd had for freshman English, she said, "Admit it — you have a crush on him." (I did but *Jeeeez!*)

I don't remember a single element of any tort. But I do recall the smooth, obscenely long faux wood tables set up in San Francisco's Moscone Center when I took the multi-day bar exam. I remember carrying my belongings — extra pencils, erasable pens — in the required plastic baggies. I remember the '80's-style overly baggy sweatshirt I wore for all three days of the exam, even though it was already 1993.

Sometimes pop culture does the best job translating complex thoughts and feelings into understandable concepts that resonate. For example, the 2015 Pixar movie "Inside

Out" helped me understand my memory. In the film, characters called "Mind Workers" pick certain memories off a shelf and toss them into the "Memory Dump," an abyss for unwanted or unnecessary memory orbs that are soon forgotten. An experience is more likely to avoid the Memory Dump — to become a long-term memory — if it's emotional or significant. It's akin to what Maya Angelou famously said: "[P]eople will forget what you said, people will forget what you did, but people will never forget how you made them feel."

That's why I remember the exact expression of my daughter, at age three, describing herself as "just a happy girl," and why I can still feel the shameful flush of my cheeks when a college friend (appropriately) chewed me out for betraying a confidence. But I have to check the dashboard every time I fill up gas to see which side the pump is on for the car I've driven for three years.

Experts understand that memory is even more complicated when it relates to trauma. Turning again to pop culture, Lady Gaga explained it spectacularly when she spoke to Stephen Colbert: "If someone...experiences trauma...it's biology that...the brain changes. And literally, what it does, is it takes the trauma and it puts it in a box, and it files it away and shuts it so that we can survive the pain. It also does a lot of other things. It can cause body pain. It can cause baseline elevations in anxiety. It can cause complete avoidance of even wanting to remember or think about what happened to you."

A 2014 Time Magazine story titled "*Why Rape and Trauma Survivors Have Fragmented and Incomplete Memories*" similarly noted that trauma survivors will remember some aspects of the experience in "exquisitely painful detail," but they will remember other aspects "not at all, or only in jumbled and confused fragments."

All of this is true, and is scientific. But it creates a two-fold problem, one related to the notion, emerging in popular culture, of "lived experience." First, as a 2021 *Psychology Today* article noted, someone's depiction of their own lived experience is not, by definition, subject to dispute. Rife with anecdotal evidence, eyewitness unreliability, and unconscious motivation, lived experience may be self-serving or even wrong. Second, gaslighting includes shifting blame, denying wrongdoing, rewriting history and minimizing someone's thoughts and feelings. The term originates from the 1930's play-turned-film Gaslight in which a husband emotionally abuses his wife by surreptitiously changing the intensity of gas lights in their home when she's alone. He insists she's imagining it, along with other household incidents he's behind, making her doubt her own memory. His goal is to have her institutionalized as "crazy" so he can steal from her. Gaslighting is a powerful tool of psychological abuse employed precisely to make a person question their own judgment, their own *lived experience.*

Indeed, partway through this project, I had an epiphany. I grasped why I insisted on approaching my Big Law story as a reporter, embarking on hours of interviews with former Schiffer Mulligan colleagues, and then devoting a significant portion of this book to partial transcripts of those interviews. I grasped why I consulted law professors and other experts, getting their professional assessment of my experience. I grasped why I finally dug out primary sources from The File that I'd kept but hadn't looked at for 30 years. I grasped why I structured this story akin to a lawyer prosecuting a case: here's what happened, here's documentary evidence and eye-witness testimony, here's an assessment from third-party experts. My method — using interviews and primary source materials in addition to my recollections — is akin to playwright Anna Deavere Smith's distinctive "verbatim" or "documentary" approach to theater in her plays Twilight: Los Angeles, 1992 (about the Rodney King riots) and The Ghost of Slavery (about slavery and the criminal justice system).

The epiphany: *If I wrote a purely personal tale, no one,* I feared, *would believe me.*

This is what it takes to tell the truth in cases like mine, a tale of micro-harassments and subtle undermining. If I don't incontrovertibly "prove" it, I feared, the wrongness of it all won't be clear.

My story is not mine alone, just like Kelli's is not just hers. Lewinsky's experience, as singular as it was, is, in reality, a dime a dozen. Chanel Miller being violated twice — once, being sexually assaulted by Stanford swimmer Brock Turner (who was found guilty on three felony counts but was released after serving only three months of a six-month sentence), and then again by those strangers who derided her online for being blackout drunk on the Stanford campus — was high profile but also, sadly, very, very common.

My favorite college professor used to say, "You can see the world in a grain of sand." In other words, this story is not merely my own personal tale of woe but is *emblematic* of what women — including female lawyers — have long endured in the workplace. While my experience happened in a California law office, versions of it have played out in nearly every industry around the world.

This book is not a personal vendetta. It's a microscope, a mirror — of the legal profession, of the workplace at large, of our culture.

If you, too, have experienced subtle misogyny, a hostile work environment, workplace bullying, or institutional gaslighting, *I see you.* I hope this story shows that you are not or were not alone. We didn't have hashtags to find each other in 1993. But it's not too late to gain solace — maybe even power — in learning that you're part of a community.

For me, it all began when I was 24. Like most young adults, I was eager for belonging, identity, self-worth...and love.

A Memory

It came back to me
not in the way
a thing might be returned
to its rightful owner
but like dance music
traveling in the dark
from one end
of a lake to the other.

— Billy Collins, *Musical Tables*

Chapter Three

1992 - Two Years Before the Jasper Brook Memo

"I could look at this face and listen to this voice for the rest of my life."

I was 24, eating creamy fettuccine in a Beverly Hills restaurant, surrounded by beautiful people and sitting across from a funny, charismatic man who'd flown hundreds of miles just to spend time with me.

It was 1992, my third year of law school. The previous summer, I'd had a successful stint as a summer associate in the San Francisco office of Schiffer Mulligan. I became friends with cool, smart and fun junior associates like Scott, Max, Tim, Kimberly and Denise. Some of those associates gave me work assignments. Some took me and the two other summer associates to lunch to make us feel welcome and talk to us about the operations and culture of a big law firm. I did well at Schiffer Mulligan (then Schiffer, Mulligan, Hamlin & Raptor) and accepted a permanent offer of employment to join the firm as an associate attorney in the litigation department in the fall of 1993 after graduation and the bar exam. (I also received a permanent job offer from the Los Angeles office of Orrick, the firm I worked at the summer between my first and second years of law school, the firm at which I wrote the memo that Jon Streeter wildly praised in his note to the head of that summer associate program. Because I wanted to return to the Bay Area, where I grew up and went to college, I chose to accept the offer from Schiffer Mulligan in San Francisco.)

Schiffer was — and still is — a top California-based law firm with hundreds of lawyers. The summer between my second and third years of law school, I worked in the San Francisco office, which then was home to about 40 lawyers. During that summer, I'd heard a lot about Mike, a guy in the summer associate class one year ahead of me who was spending that summer of '92 studying for the grueling California bar exam and would join the San Francisco office as an associate attorney the fall before I would, the fall that I was back at law school for my third and final year. It was clear from the frequency and affection with which partners and associates referenced him that summer that everyone at Schiffer Mulligan loved Mike.

During winter break of my third year of law school in Los Angeles, at the end of 1992, I was back home in the Bay Area for the holidays. I decided to spend an afternoon of my vacation visiting the offices of Schiffer Mulligan to say hi to the lawyers I'd worked and socialized with the summer before and who would become my full-time colleagues after I graduated from law school in June and took the bar exam in the summer. While visiting the Schiffer Mulligan's office during that December, I finally met Mike for myself as he was now a full-blown attorney in his first year of practice. Outgoing and friendly, with a booming voice, Mike did, indeed, seem like a great guy. He had charisma, what the kids today call "rizz."

I was predisposed to be attracted to Mike for other reasons: he was tall, self-assured and funny, all qualities I was historically attracted to in men, especially the funny part. For me, funny could override looks any day. I laugh easily and loudly. My particular aphrodisiac is smart, clever humor.

Mike was nice enough looking — not a hunk but decently attractive, with dark hair, a contagious, easy laugh and a wide smile. (A few months later, my college friend Terry saw a photo of me and Mike on the refrigerator in my apartment and spat out, "My God, that guy has a huge mouth!" In hindsight, I realize this was true both literally and figuratively. Was the Universe — through Terry — trying to warn me?)

When you're Jewish, there's something, too, about meeting another Jew. Sometimes you don't even need the fact confirmed — you just *know* — because there's a mysterious kind of instant affinity. Jews can "pass" as mainstream, but you can also just sense when someone is really more like you than the mainstream. This is especially true when you're in an environment that is decidedly not Jewish, as Schiffer Mulligan was in the early '90's.

I happened to know for a fact that Mike was Jewish. And like most Jews who meet each other for the first time, there was that immediate comfort and familiarity. I've also always had a thing for nerdy Jewish guys. Ross from "Friends" (note, not David Schwimmer, who played him) remains one of my biggest TV crushes.

Not long after that pop-in visit to Schiffer Mulligan during winter break, I was back in L.A. for my final semester of law school. And...my computer died. This was back in the day so it may have even been the behemoth Apple IIc desktop I'd been using since college.

Because I would need a new computer only a little bit for law school but much more for life after law school, I wondered if there was a certain type of computer I should get that would be compatible with what I'd be using at Schiffer Mulligan. (Again, this was 1993 so there was no Google Docs, no Cloud.)

I called Mike, who was a new first-year associate, to ask what he recommended I get. First-year associates are the lowest attorneys in the large law firm power structure, receiving work assignments from more experienced associates and partners. First-years have the lowest billable hour rates so they do the grunt work — mind-numbing document review, tedious legal research — as they learn the art and craft of lawyering from the more senior attorneys. I figured that Mike, who was in the first-year associate position I'd soon have, could tell me first-hand what home computer would serve me best for the kind of work I'd begin doing in the same department the next fall. Not surprisingly, he could not have been more charming on the phone. We had one of those conversations that was easy and fun. And he told me what kind of computer to get.

The next thing I knew — or at least the next thing in my memory — we were in regular contact and before too long he was flying down to L.A. to visit me. I remember him telling me (after the fact) that he'd had a long conversation with Patrick, a fellow associate, about where to place his overnight bag when he entered my apartment, which I found so endearing. He confessed later that he *wanted* to sleep with me but didn't want me to think that he *presumed* he'd sleep with me. So, as prearranged with Patrick, Mike placed his overnight bag down with a flourish in my living room just inside the front door. But, of course, we slept together. Our interpersonal chemistry was electric — and undeniable.

I've always been terrible at flirting because I leave nothing to the imagination. I can have deep, honest conversations — friends have told me that they feel safe, even compelled, to reveal secrets to me — but I suck at rom-com-worthy banter. I smile easily, not coyly. It's against my nature to be anything but myself. I've always been a what-you-see-is-what-you-get person, completely lacking both a facade or a hard shell. I *want* to be cool, badass, sarcastic, even a bit cynical but I'm none of those things. At 24, especially, I was not fierce or mysterious. I was simply...nice.

One afternoon in college, I was hanging out in a sorority sister's room. Callie was beautiful and popular, both within the sorority and on campus generally. Callie's boyfriend — also hot and popular — called on the phone. With a shake of her head, Callie whispered to her roommate, who'd answered the phone, "Tell him I'm not here." Callie's roommate executed this lie with an ease that proved it wasn't the first time Callie made her boyfriend...wait. Reflecting my shock, my jaw hung, but I quickly snapped it shut so as not to reveal the inner workings of my brain. It never in a million years would have occurred to me to not make myself available for a call from a boyfriend, especially a hot, popular boyfriend. The moment sticks so crisply in my mind because it was then that I grasped that there's a distinct difference between women like Callie and women like me. Like her, I could get *into* a top sorority on campus. But I lacked the confidence, the "X factor" that pushed girls like Callie to the upper, upper echelons of the campus social scene. She had — and I lacked — what Sean Hayes, Jason Bateman and Will Arnett refer to on their Smartless podcast as "sexy indifference." Aside from mascara and lipstick, any sexiness I possessed — then and now — was not by design.

I'd had several boyfriends before, but from the earliest days, my relationship with Mike felt different and special, more grown up. I laughed so much during Mike's first visit to see me in Los Angeles. He told me later that weekend that it was during that Beverly Hills dinner on Friday night that he'd had that defining "look at this face/listen to this voice" thought. I'll never forget those words and the earnest and eager way he revealed to me how he was feeling. He liked the real me. And I liked him.

Some might suggest that I had a mighty high opinion of myself to unquestioningly believe what Mike said, what others might intuitively sense was obvious hyperbole. After all, we didn't know each other well yet. But it was actually quite the opposite. I don't manipulate or play games. I put on zero pretense. Playing hard to get was simply against my constitution. I could never be anything but transparently myself — agreeable and open. I was young enough and inexperienced enough to assume that people I was drawn to took the same approach to interpersonal relationships.

Also, my self-esteem actually wasn't great. I'd always succeeded — in school, in social settings — but often by the skin of my teeth or because of outsized striving, neither of which served to engender confidence in myself. I deeply identified with what June Carter Cash once said: "I'm just trying to matter." I latched eagerly right onto Mike's words without an ounce of cynicism. Where were the critical thinking skills I'd honed in law school?

All I know is that I was deliriously happy, and you can't help how someone makes you feel. From then on, Mike was my boyfriend. I'd finally found my person.

I discovered in a keepsake box a card that accompanied a box of See's candy Mike sent me in February 1993, probably for Valentine's Day. There was also a letter with "The Keeper" on the return address, a reference to what my mother said about Mike after she met him, that he was "a keeper." In *my* address on that same envelope, "Esq." (the signifier for Esquire, a lawyer) was crossed out after my name with a little note that read, "I forgot only *I* could use this." At the time, I thought that his teasing me that he was a licensed lawyer when I had not yet graduated from law school was funny. Only now, after everything that happened later, I see the insensitive edge to his joke. But at the time, I found it — and him — charming.

Another card he sent, dated March 13, 1993 (a few days before we planned to see each other) featured a picture of Jerry Seinfeld, one of his heroes and one of those nerdy Jewish guys he knew I found attractive. On the cover, the card read: "Women go after doctors like men go after models. They want someone with knowledge of the body." Once opened, it read, "We just want the body." Inside, Mike wrote:

"Dear Erin, You know that I must be feeling awfully good about us to be willing to take the risk of sending you a card with a guy on it with whom you are 'enamored.' If, however, you want to send me a card with a picture of somebody with whom I am enamored you may use any number of those pictures in your apartment. Mike p.s. No funny stuff with pictures of your cat! p.p.s. Anticipation for Thursday is running *very high*!"

We also spent a lot of time on the phone. I'd lay on my very '90's green and cream striped couch while Mike told me stories that made me laugh while my cat Mensch played nearby or purred on my chest. I'd adopted Mensch in the fall of 1992 when he was a five-month-old kitten. Solid grey with green eyes, Mensch got his name (a Yiddish descriptor of someone supportive, calm and helpful, someone with decency and integrity, the kind of man Jewish mothers want their daughters to marry) on the drive home from the adoption center when he purred non-stop from his cardboard carrier, clearly grateful to have found a forever home. Mensch lived up to his name, always snuggly and affectionate. He purred whenever he laid eyes on me.

Details about my relationship with Mike are scattered and blurry, partly because it's been 30 years, partly because of the trauma that followed and partly, too, because I was in those delicious, early days of a relationship. To me, Mike was both so delightfully new, a person with seemingly endless opportunities to laugh with, and also someone I was instantly comfortable with. The relationship was consuming and intense, and I presumed that was simply how it felt when one finally connected with a true love. Our relationship felt buzzy and prized — like a secret. I felt loved and I felt lucky.

He met my parents. I met his. He met my sister. I met his brother. In the passenger seat of his car as we drove from his Marina apartment to meet his dad for dinner at

Gaspare's pizza on Geary Boulevard, I remember feeling so *grown up*. I imagined us driving everywhere together — to parties and parent-teacher conferences, to work and family gatherings.

I was delighted to be wildly loved and in love. My early 20's had felt like musical chairs — everyone was pairing up with a partner and I hadn't even known we were playing. With Mike, I finally found my own matching chair.

We went to basketball games and dive bars. We doubled-dated with Patrick — another associate at the firm — and his girlfriend Sandy, a Schiffer Mulligan staff person who I'd befriended during my summer internship at the firm. The peak of our relationship, which may have actually been an apt metaphor given how young and immature we both were, was a day at Disneyland when he was in L.A. visiting me for a weekend. The sun was warm and high in the sky. We put law school study groups and boring first-year associate assignments aside for the day. We almost wet our pants while laughing on Space Mountain and the Matterhorn. We ate junk food and got hysterical when we'd see little kids crying, joking to each other in a Seinfeld-esque way, "Kid, buck up. It doesn't get any better than where you are now."

One night a few weeks later, we were talking on the phone when someone buzzed Mike's apartment unexpectedly. He asked me to hold on while he answered. When he came back to the phone, he was rushed and distressed. "It's Nicole," he said, referring to his most recent ex-girlfriend. "She's really upset and she's outside. I'm going to go talk to her."

"Okay," I said hesitantly from my apartment 300 miles away.

"Erin," he said, earnestly, "I'm crazy about you. I'll call you back."

Naively, I did not see a hysterical ex-girlfriend showing up at his door unannounced as a red flag. Rather, it reinforced my feeling lucky to be with someone so desirable. I had no idea that before too long I'd be next. I was "love blind," which "Ted Lasso" character Keeley Jones described as "an emotional version of color blindness where a person interprets red flags as giant, green just-fucking-go-for-it flags."

In groups, Mike was performative. He was loud and inordinately loved being the center of attention. He did hilarious bits recounting conversations he had with his law school roommate Constantine, complete with his thick Greek accent. Mike relished the attention he got being a disheveled wreck the morning after he pulled his first all-nighter at Schiffer Mulligan. He seemed to love Passover because he was the only lawyer in the office who would not eat leavened bread and he could make a big show of the salads he had to eat for lunch for eight straight days.

Mike was also obsessive. He loved the 10,000 Maniacs' cover of "Peace Train" so much that he made an entire cassette tape of just that one song playing over and over and over. (When I made him a mix tape, his response was to tease me for misspelling "suprise" in the accompanying card.)

Like me, Mike grew up in the Bay Area. We both went to college at UC Berkeley, but he was a year older than me and, amidst the tens of thousands of students there, we never crossed paths. Mike and his younger brother were raised primarily by his mom. His relationship with his father, a difficult Israeli man, seemed strained.

Mike was persuasive. And he was especially persuasive with me.

When I expressed concern about the fact that in just a few short months, we'd be working together not only in the same law office but in the same department, he assured me that there was nothing to worry about, that our relationship was for the long haul.

It wasn't prudent to fall in love with a colleague at the launch of my professional career, one that I'd spent three grueling years preparing for. But I already had the job. Plus, our peers were matching up, moving in together, getting engaged. Mike and I were simply going along with the flow of traffic, I reasoned. I was in love and I trusted my partner when he insisted that working at the same firm would be fine.

Plus, if I was forced to give one up, which would I pick?

The job I'd worked so hard to get?

The man I loved who insisted we'd spend the rest of our lives together?

The definitive answer was neither.

Before I met Mike, my plan was to stay in Los Angeles after graduation and study for the bar exam alongside my tight squad from law school. We'd been studying together for three years, sharing outlines and supporting each other through professors' Socratic method grilling and grueling final exams that determine one's entire grade in a course. But a couple of months into our relationship, Mike said that he'd miss me too much to wait until mid-summer for me to finally move to San Francisco. To oblige, I'd have to re-work my plans, including giving notice at my apartment, figuring out a different bar review course location, and moving all of my belongings immediately after graduation.

Despite the logistical headaches, it was an easy decision for a few reasons. First, I was *in love*. I wanted to be closer to Mike. We'd only been dating a few months but already the long-distance thing — this was years before texting and FaceTime, and even before email

— was getting old. Also, after three years, I was done with Los Angeles, especially the traffic. A simple errand to get a shoe repaired took well over an hour. I had to go grocery shopping at 8 a.m. to ensure I'd get a parking space. I was over it.

Mike *also* persuaded me that we should move in together. We were mid-20's and in love. My friends were moving in with their boyfriends and even getting married. It was, I figured, just what you did. So I agreed. Things were moving fast, for sure, but we were in love. I was ready to start my life in all ways — as a professional, as part of an adult couple.

Mike's apartment was small and didn't allow pets so we decided to rent a new apartment together. At that point, I was still in Los Angeles and Mike was swamped with the work of being a first-year associate. So my parents took a couple of weekends to look at Marina apartments for us. Mike already lived in the Marina and we both loved the neighborhood. Situated on the Bay, near the foot of the Golden Gate Bridge, the Marina was *the* neighborhood for yuppies. Early 20th century apartment buildings were scattered along streets near the fun commercial hub of Chestnut Street. Chestnut featured everything from yoga studios to pubs, bookstores to movie theaters, brunch spots to The Gap. My parents found a large, pet-friendly one-bedroom apartment on the residential end of Chestnut Street, just a few blocks from Mike's current place on Fillmore Street. It was in a beautiful old Spanish-style building that featured hardwood floors, an enormous living room and lots of closet space. Because San Francisco apartments went like hotcakes, especially in the Marina, my parents signed the lease on our behalf the very afternoon they saw it.

While many details of our relationship have faded with time, I say with 100 percent certainty that both of those developments — my moving to San Francisco early and our renting an apartment together — were *Mike's idea*. Admittedly, both were easy asks because I was eager and willing to move our relationship at the pace he'd set. But *he* was the driving force.

Towards the end of my final semester of law school, I was back in the Bay Area visiting Mike. We'd signed up for the legendary Bay to Breakers wacky foot race. It turned out to be the very first time I sensed a distance in him. We didn't talk much during the race, instead we just made random comments about the funky costumes and naked runners. After crossing the finish line, we could not for the life of us find a cab to get back to his place in the Marina and every single MUNI bus was packed. We decided to walk another mile and a half — in addition to the more than seven from the race itself — to his dad's house in the Outer Sunset district. We were exhausted. From there, we were finally able to call a cab. While we waited, Mike showed me with pointed sarcasm that his father was so protective of his new kitchen counters that he placed close to 10 cutting boards over every single counter surface. It was the only joke he made the entire day.

I spent those last few weeks in L.A. wishing that time would move faster, that I could get to San Francisco and *start my life*. I'd lay in bed at night and watch the numbers on my digital clock move, willing them to speed up.

Finally, a few weeks after the Bay to Breakers and days after my graduation, I packed up my apartment in L.A. and drove with Mensch and my dad, who'd come to help me, to San Francisco. I dropped my dad off at home on the Peninsula and continued straight north to Mike's apartment because the lease on our shared Chestnut Street apartment hadn't started yet.

Mensch, still very much a kitten at less than a year old, was terrified. Mike didn't seem like himself but instead distinctly irritated by my presence. I remember him brusquely shoving Mensch off the kitchen table. (In hindsight, I should have put an end to the relationship right then or at the very least shown some backbone by putting my foot down. I understand not wanting an animal on a table, but Mike knew how deeply I loved Mensch. Shoving him was not okay.) I remember Mike leaving for the bulk of the next day to "do laundry" at either his mom's or his dad's house. Before he left that morning, he teased me about how I looked sleeping on my stomach with the soles of my feet delicately crossed. It was the last light moment I remember between us.

The actual breakup happened in June after all of my belongings arrived at the Chestnut Street apartment. Mike never moved in. He asked to come over one evening "to talk." Deep down, I knew something was wrong. But I also couldn't grasp that our intense connection, his professions of love, could suddenly amount to nothing.

When he arrived, he looked profoundly uncomfortable, as if he was in the throws of a bad case of food poisoning.

Whatever he said was crafty and vague — something I couldn't dispute — along the lines of "this isn't working for me." I do distinctly remember that he offered to pay for some of the pricey Chestnut Street rent until I began work at Schiffer Mulligan in October.

I felt not anger but sheer, profound disbelief. Have you ever watched "The Bachelor" during one of those seasons when, at the end, the man picks the absolute wrong woman between the final two? And the unadulterated, bewildered confusion on the face of the woman sent home, the woman with whom he'd clearly, obviously had the stronger connection? Picture that times a thousand. We'd never once fought or otherwise had a conflict about goals or values or...anything. There was no point-of-origin to his about-face.

In those moments, I summoned all my strength and actively strived to appear reasonable amidst the abrupt, baffling end.

Maybe he'll change his mind, an inner narrator spoke to me.

Amidst my confusion about what was happening and until I could make sense of what I was actually feeling, I tried to strike a delicate balance, to project appropriate disappointment but not irrational anger. I was teary but didn't weep.

If I express my pain, it'll push him away for good.

As I watched him walk out of the apartment and down the hallway, lit by 1920's iron sconces, his posture reflected profound relief.

This was more than just an abrupt breakup. I'd drastically changed my living situation because of Mike. (Had *he* even given notice at his apartment?) And he was not simply a former boyfriend I could get over privately, in my own time. I'd trusted Mike when he'd said that our working together in the same department at the same law firm would never be an issue given the strength of our relationship. Before long, I'd be forced to see him *every day* at work. I might even have to work *with* him.

Perhaps the cruelest part of the breakup and its timing was this: my job offer at Schiffer Mulligan hinged on my passing the California bar exam, which was coming up in a few short weeks in July. One part of Schiffer Mulligan's machismo was that ever since the San Francisco office was founded, not one single lawyer from that outpost had failed the bar exam. In addition to the fact that I was studying for the bar during a sudden, unkind breakup, Schiffer Mulligan's prideful statistic added unbearable pressure. Having taken the bar exam just the summer before, Mike well knew that the passage rates in California hovered around 50 percent. It was a crap shoot whether someone — no matter how smart or well-educated — would pass even when all was going right in that person's life. And suddenly, in my life, things were going very, very wrong.

Could I have imagined everything?

Was he lying when he said he wanted to spend the rest of his life together?

What had I done to trigger this abrupt shift?

Over and over in my head, I replayed our months of interactions, feeling insecure and wobbly. I was gutted, heartbroken in a way I'd never experienced.

I've always had inordinate difficulty letting relationships go, friendship or otherwise. If another person and I invested time in each other, I remained committed to it even if we moved on to different schools or jobs or cities. To me, if we didn't stay in touch, then that meant our time together wasn't real, had actually been time wasted, something I couldn't abide. In her memoir, *I'm Glad My Mom Died*, former child actor Jennette McCurdy captured this feeling perfectly when she wrote about what happens to TV set friendships after a show ends: "[L]ittle by little, you realize you start talking less and less to the people you thought you were so intimate with. Until you don't talk to them at all anymore. And it makes you wonder if you were ever really intimate with them in the first place or if it was all just a facade. If the connections were as temporary as the sets they were made on."

I've long been commended for being a great correspondent (all the way back to the days of snail mail — ask my best summer camp friend), a loyal friend. Later, I would come to understand that these qualities could sometimes be compulsion-based, a way to prove to myself that the time invested in a friendship was well spent. One law colleague I was mildly friendly with moved back to Pennsylvania after a few months in San Francisco. I later called her a few times to check in after she moved away to see how she was. I only stopped making the effort after she once answered my call with a surprised, sardonic laugh — like, "why are you bothering?" It takes some actual unkindness like that for me to finally let go.

I love food and am an emotional eater. Typically, when I'm upset, I eat. I never struggled with under-eating — except during those summer months in 1993. This was a whole different kind of upset. I had zero appetite. The thought of putting food in my mouth, of chewing, of swallowing, made me sick, actually made me gag. I'd never experienced anything like it before or since. Given my love of food, my inability to eat was a strong measure of how much emotional pain I was in. Every once in a while that summer I'd get a small craving for something sweet. I'd eat half a gallon of mint chip ice cream right out of the tub but that would be the only thing I could stomach for the whole day. To this day, one bite of Dreyer's bright green mint chip ice cream takes me right back to that solitary summer.

I somehow managed to drag myself from my new home on Chestnut Street to the bar review course at Hastings College of the Law (now called UC College of the Law, San Francisco) in the Tenderloin. Among the hundreds of other attorney hopefuls, I knew not a soul. Meanwhile, my beloved law school friends were studying together in Los Angeles. My high school and college friends were either working full-time or in graduate school themselves and none of them could relate to the grueling, monumental task I had to accomplish before I could work as a licensed lawyer. Thank God for my cat Mensch because, in addition to being brokenhearted, I was very, very lonely.

I followed the bar prep course's prescriptions to the letter, which included hours upon hours of memorizing outlines in subjects as diverse as trusts and estates, criminal law, property, and constitutional law. I also used an old-fashioned tape recorder to capture myself reading my outlines out loud into cassette tapes, which I then played whenever I was in the car. During the actual exam, I sometimes remembered where I'd been driving when I recalled in my mind my own voice laying out the elements of a particular tort.

I took the three-day exam at San Francisco's Moscone Center, alongside thousands of other attorney hopefuls. I knew no one. Each morning, I prayed a huge atheist prayer that there would be a constitutional law essay question but not a property law one. During breaks, I sat outside alone. Typical of San Francisco in the summer, the sky was gloomy and overcast. Each evening, I was emotionally and intellectually exhausted but slept poorly. When it was over, I couldn't celebrate with my law school friends because they were all in Los Angeles. I had no idea if I'd passed or tanked.

A few weeks later, just a couple of months before I was scheduled to officially start work, I got a distressing glimpse of what was to come at Schiffer Mulligan. I learned that the firm hosted a social gathering at an Oakland A's game and I was *the only person* out of the incoming class of first-year associates and current attorneys who wasn't invited. My fellow incoming first-year associates, Vanessa and Brian, had attended, enabling them to make connections with lawyers who'd soon be giving them assignments. This was not an administrative oversight — there were only three of us incoming first-years. Someone — whether at Mike's direction or merely because of our breakup — had deliberately not included me. This hurt my feelings, of course. But, worse, it impacted my ability to begin building relationships with more senior lawyers who could give me work assignments.

I hadn't even started working at the firm yet. What, exactly, had I done to be excluded from firm events?

Chapter Four

1993

My professional career began in a world that's vastly different than it is today. Many of the events of 1993 and 1994 seem almost quaint by current standards of school shootings, fentanyl overdoses, below-the-belt campaigning and the global devastation caused by Covid-19.

During my first year as a law firm associate:

Bill Clinton was serving his first term as president. Former San Francisco mayor Dianne Feinstein was serving in her first year as senator. Gavin Newsom, 26, was opening wineries and small hotels.

San Francisco, still primarily famous for its role in the Gold Rush, had not yet experienced its explosion as a tech Mecca, and neither had Silicon Valley, its neighbor region 45 minutes south. In 1993, Mark Zuckerberg was nine years old.

The Golden State Warriors' record was 50-32. Stephen Curry was five.

San Francisco's very first Starbucks, on Union and Laguna Streets, celebrated its one-year anniversary.

We used pencils to keep track of friends' numbers in a physical address book. For critical information, we consulted yellow pages, paper maps and Thomas Guides. Used solely by the rich and famous, cell phones were humongous. Email was brand new and addresses often had strings of more than 10 characters before the "@." Casual Friday was just barely emerging, but at only the most progressive companies.

Clarence Thomas was newly serving on the US Supreme Court after Anita Hill, a young African-American law professor, was peppered with questions by an all white, all male Judiciary Committee during additional confirmation hearings held after her allegations of Thomas's misconduct became public. The Judiciary Committee declined to question corroborating witnesses who were willing to testify.

Big Law, as it's now called, was squarely ensconced in compulsion culture in the 1990's. Lawyers beat their chests about how many hours they billed, about how late they stayed at the office. (Remote work was most definitely not a thing as integrated computer networks were barely around in the early '90's, and if you listened to a colleague's voicemail, that meant that you were actually in your office with your physical phone because that was the only way to retrieve those messages.)

In elementary terms, law firm partnerships are like a pie. If you're admitted to the partnership, you're expected to contribute capital as part of your ownership in the business. But the upside is that you also share in the profits. Typically, the pie isn't divvied up in even slices — the more income a partner generates, either by number of hours billed or number of client matters brought into the firm, the bigger the slice. As a result, there's significant gatekeeping in the legal profession. Law firm partners who bring in lots of business are referred to as "rainmakers" and they're given lots of deference from the other partners.

Clients are usually billed by the hour, in 15- or six-minute increments. Pie division ranges from firm to firm — some structured in compensation tiers and others through complicated formulas that factor in business generation and hours billed — and is usually decided by a powerful compensation committee. The partnership compensation structure has a huge effect on the culture of the firm. Do partners hoard or share clients? Do competitive partners secretly monitor the billable time of their colleagues or do they assume that the compensation allocation is fair? Associates — attorney worker bees at the firm who are not partners — have a strict and intense minimum billable hour requirement to justify their high salaries and to stay on the partnership track.

Billing the required minimum — 1,900 hours a year at that time at Schiffer Mulligan — was a non-negotiable in Big Law. Neither professional training nor required pro bono hours (volunteer hours for charitable organizations) counted towards that hefty minimum. Typically, eight hours in the office resulted in a mere five or six billable hours. Not meeting the hours requirement was grounds for termination. Getting meaty assignments from partners and senior associates was absolutely critical.

By the early 1990's, women were graduating from law school in equal numbers to men. I thought that merely graduating from law school meant that I had an equal chance of succeeding in Big Law as my male counterparts. But the sheer numbers of women entering the profession were not enough to dismantle the concrete systems set up precisely to perpetuate the dominance of white men in law firm partnerships. Law firm *clients* were still mostly men, and female lawyers were competing for work assignments from the men who controlled those assignments.

***

As my start date at Schiffer Mulligan grew closer, my dread and terror grew. I'd already been excluded from a baseball game that Vanessa and Brian — the other two incoming lawyers — had been invited to. I didn't know why or what other events I might have been excluded from. I was still waiting apprehensively for my bar results. I feared what it would be like to work alongside the man who broke my heart.

Before my first day at Schiffer Mulligan, the first day I'd see Mike in many months, I plucked and waxed and primped and polished. I meticulously prepared my appearance from hairstyle to pedicure to accessories. I beautified more for that first day of work at Schiffer Mulligan than I did years later for my wedding. I decided to wear one of my favorite suits, one that was feminine, more luncheon-style than business suit. It was color-blocked — mostly navy but with wide blocks of cream and dark pink — with big gold buttons.

The night before and that morning I was a wreck. My heart raced and my breath stayed short and high in my chest. I wanted to stay at home reading novels in the overly expensive apartment that Mike and I were supposed to share together, snuggled next to Mensch. But the day to begin the career I'd spent three years preparing for had finally come.

Distracted and breathing shallowly, I drove to the Embarcadero Center, a financial district complex near the waterfront built in the 1970's, comprised of several high-rises with commercial space on the lower floors and business offices on top. In the early '90's, the Embarcadero was home to places like Ann Taylor, the California Mexican food chain Chevy's and an independent bookstore that no longer exists. When I think of the Embarcadero, I conjure images of the floors, made up of concrete tiles in circular designs. That floor design traveled through Embarcadero One, Two, Three or Four and those tiles became very slippery when it rained. I remember falling at least once, and I heard rumors that the Center was constantly paying settlements to people who'd been injured that way.

I arrived at the Schiffer Mulligan offices on the 17th floor of one of the Embarcadero buildings. From the moment I got out of my car in the underground garage (Schiffer

Mulligan prided itself on being the only San Francisco firm to offer parking to associates, which was an enormous perk), I felt as if I were on stage. I could — and certainly would — run into Mike *at any moment* and I wanted that moment to go well. I wanted to pass the test. I wanted him to come crawling back, to beg my forgiveness for making a colossal mistake in breaking up with me, a mistake that could only be explained by a simple fear of commitment.

An office administrator gave me a tour of the office, all light blue and grey and pale wood. She was not so much showing me around — after all, I'd spent the previous summer interning there — but giving lawyers an opportunity to greet me, one of the three brand new first-year attorneys. When we walked down the hall where I knew Mike's office was, my breath quickened and I thought I might pass out. Still, I plastered a smile on my face and continued chatting mindlessly with the person giving the tour. As we got closer, I saw that his light was out, which I found odd. Since that was before energy-saving, motion-sensored lights, offices stayed lit even if you were up in the library or out to lunch. The tour guide approached the entryway to his office, knocked on the door jamb, and then said to herself, "Ah, that's right, he's on vacation."

All of the air left my body. But I couldn't determine if I was relieved or pissed off. After all, his absence meant I was going to have to re-do the head-to-toe primping all over again next week. On the other hand, was this a sign of respect on his part? Was he trying to give me space during the first week of my legal career? And where had he gone on vacation — *and with whom*? I felt an overwhelming urge to lie down. I needed to process it all. But I couldn't. I was starting my first real professional job. It required personal and intellectual focus.

Eventually, I was led down another hallway to what would be my office, a tiny office deep in a corner of newly annexed space on the 16th floor. I was on the same floor as Mike but as far away from him as I could be. I was also far away from the main action upstairs — reception, the library, the coffee room, many conference rooms. Vanessa and Brian, the other two first-year attorneys, were given offices up there.

In those first days of work, I learned from a couple of other associates that all summer, while I'd been studying for the bar exam, Mike had been discussing with my future Schiffer Mulligan co-workers the demise of our private relationship. And it wasn't just a one-off — it was pervasive.

I heard that Mike portrayed me to my future colleagues and superiors as a "basket case" because of our breakup. He apparently said that he'd "freaked out" when I moved to San Francisco and also that I couldn't get over him.

Although contributing a small portion of the rent had been his idea, Mike that summer had also apparently complained to colleagues about having to pay me "alimony."

A couple of associates revealed that Mike allegedly told lawyers at the firm that he was certain I'd fail the bar exam.

Because we lived five blocks apart in the Marina, we agreed during the breakup to try to stay away from each other in the neighborhood. But somehow it got around at the firm that summer that I didn't want Mike "walking down certain streets" in San Francisco.

I learned from associates that partners and associates at Schiffer Mulligan had teased Mike that summer about my impending arrival at the firm. And they allegedly asked Mike, who I — and they — knew had slept with the firm's librarian long before he met me, which one of us was better in bed.

I was astonished and profoundly hurt. The sudden breakup had been awful enough. But his talking about me and our private relationship with my future colleagues was agonizing and terrifying.

It's obvious to me now that Mike got a simple case of cold feet. He grew scared about the commitment he promised and propelled forward. We were so young, hadn't been dating that long and most of it was long distance. We both jumped the gun. He didn't want to spend the rest of his life with me after all. That, of course, was his prerogative.

I get it.

I really do.

But what I didn't understand then and what makes me livid today is why he shit-talked me to *our mutual colleagues*?

Clearly, I hadn't yet grasped just how nasty Mike could be. I still thought the whole thing was a big test that I could somehow pass. No one at the firm knew that all I'd done was simply what Mike convinced me to do. *He'd* been the one to propel the relationship forward at warp speed. *He'd* insisted we get an apartment together and, when he broke up with me out of the blue, *he'd* offered to pay a small portion of the rent for a limited time until I began earning a salary. In The File, I have photocopies of a grand total of five checks totaling a few hundred dollars.

The truth of the matter was that I *was* a basket case. Every time I left my apartment — to buy cat food at the pet store on the corner, to get groceries or even just to get some fresh air — I was shaky and nauseous, fearful that I'd run into Mike, who still lived just five blocks from me. I'd wake in the middle of the night when I should have been getting as much rest as I could during those hellacious weeks preparing for the bar exam.

I still couldn't understand Mike's swift and inexplicable turnaround, from adoring to callous indifference. As with all of my personal relationships, I'd been nothing but wholly myself with him, utterly lacking in pretense. I became obsessed with trying to know the unknowable: which Mike was the real one? If he'd cared for me even a fraction of the amount I'd thought he had, how could he participate in conversations that were hurtful to me personally and to my career? And because I was still so confused and hurt, any time I displayed even the tiniest emotional fragility at work, it only served to prove the worst characterizations about me.

I made mistakes. I fell in love. I had a tough time getting over it. I was naive. But expecting perfection from women is part of insidious gender conditioning in our culture.

***

A couple of weeks into my time at Schiffer Mulligan, I called my parents one morning in tears. In the earliest days of my professional life, I was completely discombobulated, figuring out everything from my commute to the names of partners and associates to the firm's computer system to filling out time sheets to the new vocabulary of Big Law. Trying to do all of this is overwhelming for any new lawyer and would have been challenging even if I'd never met Mike. But learning of the gossip that had run rampant during the summer and then seeing Mike every day, trying to decipher our interactions, working to maintain my composure amidst confusion and heartbreak, all while waiting for the critical results of the bar exam was too much.

"Call your doctor," my dad ordered upon hearing my distress.

The answering service woke my primary care doctor up and by the time he got on the phone, I was sobbing. It was only 7 a.m. He prescribed a quick-acting anti-anxiety medication — probably Ativan. I had long avoided taking medication — even ibuprofen — unless absolutely necessary. But I willingly dashed to the Walgreens around the corner at Divisadero and Lombard, popped the pill and somehow made it to work on time.

Mike was what I would call a street angel, house devil. To everyone else, he was gregarious and fun. To me, though, while never physically abusive, he was growing downright ugly. We didn't talk much in the office but occasionally we'd have private discussions, often at a my instigation as I was trying to sort out everything that happened and was happening. He'd tell me that I was too sensitive, that all he'd done was get out of a relationship in which he wasn't happy. He accused me of overreacting. He deflected responsibility and twisted facts.

In those first months at Schiffer Mulligan, Mike seemed to get a sick kind of pleasure in telling me negative things that other people said or thought about me. That I was even a topic of conversation at all was frightening and maddening. He reported, for example, that on my first day at the firm (when Mike himself was on vacation) that Kimberly, a senior associate, had apparently whispered to another associate, "I can't believe she wore that suit."

Chapter Five

1993

There was a clubbiness to Schiffer Mulligan's San Francisco office that colleagues I interviewed in 2023 described as "a frat," a "cast of characters," and "a bro factory."

The de facto leader of "The Club" was Ben Bucknell, a friendly, handsome guy in his late 30's. He had two young boys and a beautiful wife. I got the summer associate position at Schiffer Mulligan because of Ben. He met my parents at a party (they lived in the same mid-Peninsula town) and mentioned he was a litigator. My parents said their daughter was in law school and had just finished a successful summer associate stint at Orrick. Ben kindly gave my parents his card and suggested I call him regarding a summer job, which I did. I received a summer associate offer (a decision Ben later told me was a "no brainer") after a single interview. It was Ben who personally welcomed me into the Schiffer Mulligan fold.

We all know people like Ben — outgoing, good-looking, superficially incredibly nice. He reminds me of my next-door neighbor, who we jokingly refer to as the mayor of our street given his gregariousness, his ability to connect with every single person on the block, whether they are an octogenarian or a middle schooler. During my summer at Schiffer Mulligan, I considered Ben to be a big brother figure. He was one of the earliest attorneys hired in the San Francisco office and served as its office managing partner for several years. He eventually left the firm for a lucrative in-house general counsel position. In a Schiffer Mulligan alumni newsletter, Ben was quoted as saying, "[O]ne of the things that we most appreciate about the firm is the collegiality and environment that we worked in there." In college, Ben had been a Sigma Nu. Schiffer Mulligan became his next frat. His minions included Tim, Max, Patrick, Thane and David Powell, among others, all men.

There were many social gatherings just for The Club and that exclusivity was in no way secret or tactful. Once, David Powell, an unhappily married gossip with an unruly mop of black hair, came bounding into the library around 6 p.m. and pointed to every single attorney in the library except me and asked if they wanted to grab drinks at Harrington's, the downstairs bar. I heard from a peripheral member of The Club that Powell frequently lamented that his wife wouldn't have sex with him (to me, this underlined how profoundly idiotic Powell was; if his wife wasn't having sex with him, it was a comment on *him* and not her, so complaining about it only served to emphasize how unappealing she found him). On the rare occasions that she relented, Powell would report to his colleagues first thing the next morning, "Got laid last night." That *I* heard these things shows how prevalent these kinds of conversations were.

There was also a lot of that's-what-she-said humor a la Michael Scott. On "The Office," those jokes were funny because they were so absurd. But at Schiffer Mulligan, they were de rigueur. One friend told me that some of the male lawyers once debated which was better: "bad sex or a good dump."

In 1993, law firm lawyers were expected to stay at one firm for the bulk, if not the entirety, of their careers. Job-hopping before reaching the mid-associate level was highly unusual and raised red flags to potential employers. Big law firms were set up like exclusive Ivy League societies, with partners (owners who split what they collectively brought in) voting on who to admit into their ranks each year, a process that could be extremely undemocratic and usually exclusionary. Law partnerships then were mostly male and very, very white. Many partners were self-important, with huge egos and little humanity. One male partner I worked with ordered me to stop leaving "niceties" in voicemail messages, niceties such as "hope the trial is going well."

Law firm work was usually doled out by a tap of the shoulder from friendships that formed during casual workplace conversations. Personal connections at law firms were fostered and nurtured during the "in-between" — the drinks after work, the walks to grab a mid-day sandwich. Women often weren't part of the in-between, which could affect work assignments. That I was excluded from the firm's outing to the baseball game was not just a personal slight that hurt my feelings but eliminated an important opportunity to make connections with partners and senior associates who could dole out work that would help me meet the strict billable hour requirement.

Tim Reids was another leading member of The Club, and Ben's primary protégée. In his early 30's, Tim was a new dad at the time. He was very, very white, the beneficiary, in my opinion, of all the automatic privileges that status affords, including admission to elite schools. In The File, I found an email exchange, dated November 8, 1993, between me and Tim, who was on the firm's hiring committee. It wasn't long after I arrived at the firm, but clearly I'd already seen first-hand that the standards for white men who fit into The Club were different than for everyone else.

Me: "Is it true that this Matt Windsor character, who received & accepted our offer [to be a summer associate], had misspellings on his resume?"

Tim: "You are right. As a condition of his employment, he has to correct all of them and submit a new resume by this summer."

Me: "Why would we want someone who is not careful and thorough enough to proofread his own resume? What made him so attractive that the firm could overlook his carelessness?"

Tim: "He's a very handsome guy. He went to the same school I did. Enough said."

Me: "Forgive me if I don't think it's funny. I think it's sad that the firm would overlook carelessness in order to perpetuate the Old Boy's Club that is so prevalent here. I interviewed some really outstanding individuals that would have done fantastic work here and I wonder if they didn't get offers b/c they wouldn't fit into the chummy boy's culture here. I know that this isn't your fault (so don't think I'm lashing out at you in particular) but it's frustrating that the one thing that sometimes makes it uncomfortable to work here is going to be perpetuated by the summer program."

Sadly, the exchange ended with me sending a follow-up email an hour or so later, an apology, which I jokingly signed Susan Faludi (the feminist writer, who was popular at the time).

In uncovering The File, I see that I did raise the misogyny I felt at Schiffer Mulligan. But it might have been because of my straightforward nature rather than bravery because I quickly backed down. I silenced myself for fear of losing my job or being labeled humorless, which would further distance me from The Club.

That, unfortunately, was part of my problem. Mike was positively beloved by The Club. His nickname was 'Baum, an affectionate diminutive of Davenbaum, his last name. In Mike's *first year* at Schiffer Mulligan, he was asked to serve as the Master of Ceremonies at the firm holiday party. One person remembered him as The Club's "mascot."

Not one person at Schiffer Mulligan ever asked *me* what had happened with Mike. Not one person ever asked if everything Mike had been blabbing about all summer was true. Standing up for myself seemed pointless when I was up against Schiffer Mulligan's golden boy. The Club being all men meant that, by definition, I simply would never be accepted. But I didn't understand that in the fall of 1993. Joining a firm was joining a new community. Mike or no Mike, I wanted to belong.

On the HBO show "Hacks," 20-something Ava says to 60-something Deborah, "I've realized that sometimes I conflate the rush I feel when a man shows interest in me with actual feelings of attraction, which makes sense because it feels good to get attention from the group that's held up as, like, the leader gods of society or whatever."

When I first heard these words, my heart stopped. I'd never conceptualized gender and sexual dynamics in this way. I'd never questioned how this constant assessment by men — perceived or real — affected my self-image and self-worth. I mentioned it to my 20-year-old daughter, who responded swiftly, knowingly, "Yup. The male gaze."

I'd never heard the term, which I now know describes society's portraying and looking at women in a way that empowers men and diminishes women. Importantly, women, too, internalize this sexist, patriarchal and misogynistic gaze, which profoundly affects how they feel about themselves and other women. Blindly accepting this male paradigm, this gender socialization is probably why I was so eager to get "in" with The Club even when it was obvious they'd never accept me. I wanted to be liked and welcomed. Having an important job among men was not enough for me. Even 30 years later, I only primped for video calls with former male colleagues from Schiffer Mulligan until I realized what I was doing and stopped.

Once, I was in the office of a Schiffer Mulligan senior associate who I was helping with a project. He was a nice guy, definitely cool but a bit on the fringes of The Club because he focused primarily on work and then going home to his family. He liked to tease me about my unconscious habit of swiping wayward hair behind my right ear. That day, after we discussed whatever project I was working on, we were joking about something, and then he laughed and said, "Erin, sometimes you're cute and sometimes you're devastatingly cute." All day I rode high on that compliment, now an unsettling indication of Schiffer Mulligan's highly sexualized workplace both in and out of The Club.

That one compliment aside — so singular and unique in its positivity amidst the hateful things to come, but which I now see was inappropriate — the male gaze at Schiffer Mulligan in 1993 completely mutilated my sense of competence and belonging, both core components of self-esteem. If only I understood then what I know now. If only I'd been aware of the male gaze, this purely social construct. Perhaps I could have examined it and tossed it and defined my worth for myself. The problem at Schiffer Mulligan was...I cared. I had joined a new community and I wanted to belong.

There was nothing comparable to The Club for women at Schiffer Mulligan, a group where this all could have been candidly discussed and maybe even addressed. The few women in the San Francisco office were deeply ensconced in keeping their practices alive amidst billable hour and client development pressures, not to mention maternity leave and, of course, their own interactions with The Club.

Young women at other firms during that time may have had different experiences; they may have had encouragement, mentorship or even basic *interest* from more senior women. New female lawyers today may have that kind of support from senior women baked into firm administration by way of affinity groups or formal mentorship programs. But at Schiffer Mulligan San Francisco in 1993, the few female partners were decidedly uninterested in the new women at the firm, including me. As workplace bullying there grew, it was dispiriting that I could find no one — not even (perhaps even *especially*) other women — who cared.

Even if it was unconscious, The Club was committed to one version of the Mike-Erin situation and it wasn't mine. After all, I fit the prevailing narrative of the time: I was a weak, crazy woman. One reason gaslighting is so powerful is that it feeds off cultural cliches of women as emotional and crazy. I naively assumed that my eagerness and my promising legal skills — as Jon Streeter captured in that memo during my summer at Orrick — would override any negative narrative from The Club. I thought that at the very least I would get work to prove myself, that I would be mentored, taught and guided as the partner-associate structure was ostensibly set up to do. (Indeed, the "professional development" section of the website of Cravath, Swaine & Moore, arguably the nation's most prestigious law firm, states, "The relationship our associates develop with partners and the informal mentoring they receive are integral to their development as lawyers.")

According to notes in The File, I spoke to Ben in December 1993 — about two months after I started work — about the rumors and conversations I'd heard about. He assured me that the discussions about our relationship had settled down, by definition acknowledging that they had happened. He also promised to stop future conversations. Today, I'm more angry with Ben than I am with Mike. A therapist friend said that children with an abusive parent often are more mad at the other parent, the one who stood by passively. While Mike proved to be just a straight-up ass, Ben, I'd thought, was like a kindly, big brother figure. Being a partner in The Club comprised primarily of associates,

Ben — the attorney who'd hired me — was the grown up in the room. Yet he looked the other way so as not to disrupt his beloved frat. He played favorites. His management and leadership were a complete failure. He should have put a stop to conversations long before I had to complain.

To use a 2023 concept, where were the upstanders at Schiffer Mulligan? Did absolutely *no one* in The Club, not even Ben, have a conscience, have any empathy for what it was like for a 25-year-old woman to be the subject of discussions of much older, more powerful men? Upon reflection, Ben's failure to step in — whether at the outset or at the very least after I spoke to him — is appalling.

While channel surfing recently, I caught the movie "9 to 5" and watched Dolly Parton's iconic dressing down of her boss, played by Dabney Coleman, after she realizes he's been spreading false rumors about her in the office: "That's why these people treat me like some dime store floozy. They think I'm screwing the boss! And you just love it, don't you? It gives you some sort of cheap thrill....I put up with all your pinchin' and starin' and chasin' me around the desk 'cause I need this job, but this is the last straw!"

I identified with Dolly's fury about untrue office rumors. And it got me wondering not only what motivated Mike to abruptly break up with me, but to then take it a step further by badmouthing me at our mutual place of work. After all, he was already unquestionably beloved by The Club and by Schiffer Mulligan as a whole, despite the fact that he'd allegedly gotten visibly drunk at several firm events and even went on an overly extravagant $800 recruiting dinner on the firm's dime.

I pondered this recently with a friend, who, when she asked the name of this rotten ex-boyfriend of mine, discovered that she had five LinkedIn contacts in common with him, "all assholes," she reported, scrolling through the list. "He must have been afraid. You're one of the most capable people I know and you coming into the firm might have spooked him."

Power, I realize now, was mine to strive for but his to lose.

Chapter Six

1993

Early on a Saturday morning in November, about a month after I started at Schiffer Mulligan, I went — like so many aspiring lawyers did back then — to the post office to intercept my mail. Bar results were arriving that day and no one wanted to wait any extra hours for their postal carriers to deliver such vital information. This was long before applicants could simply log onto a web portal. Only about half of test-takers pass the notoriously difficult exam so results had monumental consequences.

My body buzzing, I ripped open the letter on the post office steps, spotting first that most critical of words in cases like this: "Congratulations." Against all odds, I passed the bar exam on that first try. (Spoiler: Even though I haven't practiced law in almost 30 years, I still pay annual dues to keep my bar membership — I worked too hard to let it go.) That day, I felt a mixture of pride, vindication and, most of all, sheer relief. Not only would I not be the Schiffer Mulligan lawyer to break the streak, but I wouldn't have to go through the awful process of re-studying.

In my offer letter dated Sept. 10, 1992, at the end of my summer associate stint, Ben Bucknell wrote: "It was a pleasure working with you this summer. You have a great future as a lawyer and we hope that you will be returning to Schiffer, Mulligan next year."

When I first started at Schiffer Mulligan, I was confident in my chances of becoming a successful lawyer. After all, I'd received offers at both law firms I'd spent summers at. And I had the gushing Jon Streeter memo in my back pocket. I didn't need constant, excessive praise like that, but, like any brand new lawyer, I did need guidance and basic mentoring.

Schiffer Mulligan felt like a good match, though I do remember walking down Market Street one day with a mix of partners and associates. We crossed paths with a group of men who clearly looked Jewish. After we passed them, one of the partners quipped out of the corner of his mouth, "Boy, those guys sure looked like they were from New York, didn't they?" The term "micro aggression" hadn't been coined yet. But I did feel that the comment, if not blatantly anti-Semitic, was indicative of some kind of bias.

When we were dating, Mike told me of a similar incident. Ben was gearing up a bunch of associates for work on a huge motion that required a lot of manpower. Ben stood on a chair in his office, giving them a motivational speech, and ended with, "Onward Christian soldiers! Oh, and you too, 'Baum!"

I knew that Schiffer, Mulligan, Hamlin & Raptor's nickname was Stalin, Mussolini, Hitler & Reagan for its conservative slant and notoriously white male leadership. But I also knew that in my summer class of three, two of us were women, two were people of color and one was Jewish. So, I figured the San Francisco office, at least, was enlightened.

Legal education has changed for the better since 1993, incorporating more clinical work and practical assignments. But back then, most law school graduates and newly licensed lawyers who'd just passed the bar exam had virtually no idea what they were doing. Unlike physicians, who gain practical experience during residencies and fellowships, most new lawyers didn't receive that hands-on practice. Learning from books the elements of negligence or the technical requirements of forming corporations in no way prepares new lawyers for the nitty gritty of filing motions, advising clients, tracking down reluctant witnesses, strategizing contracts clauses, etc. That's what mentors are for.

Despite my new license to practice law, I didn't yet understand the job and had no mentor to guide me. During one associate training session at the firm, someone asked me what we, as lawyers did. When called on by the leader of the training, I only half-jokingly responded, "Write memos." (In those days, a primary part of the job of new litigation associates was to thoroughly research a legal issue — using actual, physical case law books — and consolidate the analysis in a memo to the senior associate or partner on a case, who might then use parts of that memo in a motion or a brief or when talking to a client. But today, with the advent of instant communication, most clients won't pay for the hours required to research and write such memos, especially given that legal research is now all digitized.)

No one ever put my tiny contribution into context and that was evident in the way I initially filled out my billing sheets. Back then, they were actual paper logs that associates filled out to keep track of hours so the firm could ensure we were on track to meet our yearly minimum requirement of 1,900 billable hours. When I first started at the firm, I wrote entries like, "Research for memo — 2.3 hours." Eventually, a partner explained that I had to be far more explicit in my descriptions because those billing sheets were what partners used to generate bills to clients. Thus, entries should have read something like, "Researched California and federal law regarding exceptions to fair claims practices of insurance companies — 2.3 hours." I was grateful for that partner's clarification because as a first-year associate, I'd believed that my "client" was the firm's partners, my employers, rather than the big corporations who'd hired us. It was an unsophisticated assumption, but also a measure of how much I wanted to please the partners I worked for.

I could write a kick-ass memo, as Jon Streeter's note about me proved, but I wasn't yet an intuitive litigator. I still needed explicit direction and supervision, neither of which I received in those early months. First-year associates were supposed to be assigned to a partner, who would be responsible for their billable time and professional development, but I wasn't assigned a partner until almost two months after I started at the firm. He was a lateral partner, new to Schiffer Mulligan himself, and wasn't in my department. As a result, I still worked on a project-by-project basis, pulled into cases completely unfamiliar to me at the last minute. This didn't play to my strengths or work style. I'll never know whether my late assignment to an ineffective partner advisor was related to the rumors about me or simple mismanagement by the firm.

Either way, I grew more and more concerned about the lack of work I was getting. That, combined with being ostracized by The Club, made me increasingly insecure about my abilities. And then, in a self-fulfilling prophecy, my work product suffered.

I remember doing a quick research project for a notorious partner who, rumor had it, had once thrown a shoe at an associate. He and I shared a secretary and I'd long observed her terror of him. He needed the answer quickly so I dug in fast and walked into his office carrying a few casebooks. I told him what I'd found, and he responded gruffly, "You sure?"

My heart thumped and my ears rang. I held up the casebooks. "I, uh, do you want to double-check?"

He rolled his eyes. "No."

What's supposed to happen is that associates are assigned to cases that they become intimately familiar with. Not only does this system lend itself to the kind of mentoring — and confidence- and skill-building — that I was not getting, but it also eliminates the time required for the associate to get up to speed on the facts of the case and the legal issues, time that partners often have to "write off" when billing clients.

I was once asked by a senior associate I didn't know to draft a motion on a case I was not assigned to. While this kind of project does happen when last-minute needs arise, it's not optimal for the associate, the assigning attorney or the client because it requires time getting the associate familiar with the case. I wasn't given much background and it was also a new-to-me type of motion. Of course, I was willing to pitch in. I needed the hours. By that point, though, I was emotionally beat up from the rumors and inappropriate conversations I'd heard were taking place among members of The Club. And my confidence-level work-wise was low because I hadn't been formally assigned to any cases. I remember stamping DRAFT in red across the top of that motion I'd written, dropping it on the senior associate's chair on a Friday afternoon and practically running out the door so I wouldn't bump into him on his way back from the bathroom or wherever he was. I felt guilty all weekend. At the same time, because of what I'd learned about The Club's conversations about me and my private life, I felt sick most of the time I was in the office. I simply had to get away when I could so I could gather my emotional strength. Early the next week, I left voicemails for the senior associate to follow up. But I never heard another word about it.

I later came to understand — but didn't then — that much of law practice, particularly litigation, was against my constitution. I was a willing worker and a strong writer, but the nuances of litigation didn't come naturally. Once, opposing counsel called me to ask for an extension on some kind of discovery deadline. "Sure, no problem," I agreed. After I hung up, I walked down the hall to the partner's office and told him about the conversation. "You did *what*?!" he yelled. It never even occurred to me that not agreeing to the extension was in our client's best interest — it was just against my nature to deliberately try to screw the other side. (This is the same partner who chided me for leaving time-wasting niceties, like "hope the trial is going well," in my voicemail messages to him.)

On the upside, I did discover in The File the cover page of a motion for summary judgment that I'd drafted for Jasper Brook, author of the infamous 1994 memo and soon to be a huge villain in my life. He'd hand-written across the top, "Erin: This is excellent. Let's go with it." Around that same time, Brook was in the elevator with me and my dad, who'd come by to see my office, and said, unsolicited, "We're very impressed with your daughter."

These are examples of the little work that I did have. But overall, my billable hours were alarmingly low. I went to partners every week to ask for work but received almost none. The File contains pages and pages of emails I sent to partners and senior associates asking for assignments, as well as a hand-written list of days/times/partners I left voicemails for asking for projects.

To this day, it's unclear whether I was intentionally denied work because of the situation with Mike or if it was merely the result of mismanagement of my billable time by the firm leaders who were supposed to oversee the distribution of work. Either way, I was forced to sit in my office staring out the window, waiting for a partner or senior associate to call or knock on my door in response to my countless requests for assignments. I couldn't leave the office. I had to just...sit...and watch the minutes tick by. At one point, I was so frustrated I took to closing my office door and reading novels. I went through James Herriot's and Raymond Carver's entire canons while getting paid $70,000.

To someone on the outside, that might sound like an awesome boondoggle. But for me, it was demoralizing. I'd just toiled away for three years in law school, an academic endeavor that did not come easily to me. And I'd spent two summers working similarly hard to prove my abilities so that I'd get hired for my first full-time professional job. Sitting in that office paging through *novels* rather than legal casebooks or deposition transcripts was humiliating. It also drastically impacted my chances for partnership down the road.

A recurring nightmare I have features me, dressed in a suit and collecting a fat paycheck, sitting in a fancy office with absolutely nothing to do. This nightmare visits me every few months and every single time, I wake in a cloud of shame that takes several hours to shake. It's a direct reflection of my reality from 1993 to 1994. I still feel ashamed that I could not perform, could not meet my own standards of productivity.

In addition to the humiliation, not getting assignments affected my ability to learn the job. First-year litigation associates are supposed to be assigned to cases so they can learn how those cases move from the plaintiff's initial complaint all the way through trial and even appeal. First-year associates are supposed to observe and be mentored by senior associates and partners who explain — or at least model — what a litigator does. First-year associates are supposed to observe depositions, review documents, draft memos on legal theories, and help with legal research and writing for big motions. First-year associates are supposed to be assigned to an effective administrative partner, who monitors the associate's time, making sure the associate is on track to meet the minimum yearly billable hour requirement. But none of that was happening for me. I got the occasional research project on cases that I was not formally assigned to that had overflow needs. And no one was competently overseeing my time at an administrative level.

Thanks to my dad, who, in his role at a corporation, was a client at a different law firm, I *did* understand the importance of cultivating a client base. I completely understood the job security in being a "rainmaker" at the firm, in being someone who brought in new clients. Knowing this, I did my best to maximize family and friend connections from the get-go, even going so far as to set up a meeting between a cousin by marriage, who was the head of a huge construction company, and a Los Angeles-based partner in the construction law group. To me, both then and now, that seems pretty badass for a first-year associate. But there was zero recognition of this coup in any review or other informal discussions regarding my future at the firm. It wasn't until years later that I truly understood the cut-throat politics of business generation credit, which translates into actual dollars. In other words: even if the firm had gotten new work from that construction company, there's no way they would have given business generation credit to a first-year associate. Especially a woman. Especially me.

I didn't help myself by ignoring the hierarchy that was the office break room, a hierarchy that I found absurd. Situated in the center of the office's main floor, the break room had a fridge and some basic provisions like coffee and tea. (This was long before the dot-com boom, which made kombuchas and other high-end freebies commonplace even for law firms.) It was unstated but plainly understood that the break room was *for staff*. I never once saw an attorney seated at the few tables and chairs there. At most, attorneys would come in to fill up their mugs with coffee, maybe offering the secretaries, paralegals and word processors a friendly nod on their way back to their offices. Attorneys didn't bring their lunches. They went out to lunch. If they got food to-go, they'd eat in their offices, never in that break room. That division disgusted me, though, looking back, maybe it was presumptuous of me. Maybe *the staff* preferred the separation. Just like I refused to wear a little man suit on my first day as a lawyer, I flouted this unspoken division in the break room. Several times a week, I ordered a plain bowl of rice with teriyaki sauce (which was all I could stomach in those days) from the Japanese fast food place downstairs. The woman behind the counter unfailingly flashed me a sharp, annoyed look at my cheap, not-on-the-menu order. Her look mirrored the barely hidden expressions of derision from the attorneys who spotted me eating that lunch in the break room alongside staff.

Aside from the occasional fleeting verbal indications that someone liked what I'd prepared for them and one off-hand remark I heard about my earlier stint as a Schiffer Mulligan summer associate (labeling me "top of the class"), I received zero formal feedback. The exact day I hit the six-month mark at the firm, I made the first of multiple requests for my six-month review. I was deeply concerned about my lack of work and the lack of oversight of my billable time and professional development. I hadn't yet realized that there was likely a distinct connection between my lack of work and what was going on in The Club. The request yielded no review.

An October 1994 article in *American Lawyer* magazine that I found in The File reported associate feedback on the country's biggest firms. According to the article, a San Francisco mid-level associate at Schiffer Mulligan wrote, "[P]artners seem to treat associates as fungible hired help." And an L.A.-based mid-level wrote, "You couldn't pay me enough to become a partner of this bunch of socially inept, morally bankrupt stiffs."

Despite the partner mentoring system failing me and the awful antics of The Club, I still tried my hardest to succeed. In addition to setting up the client meeting for the L.A. partner, I also wrote a memo in early 1994 to Frederick Duncan, managing partner of the San Francisco office, to show that I was eager to promote the firm as a business (something at which law firms are notoriously horrible). In the memo, I explained that public relations, which was cheaper than advertising, was emerging as an effective and affordable way to let law firm clients know about new and expanding practice areas. I attached several articles about the work a particular PR company was doing for a big Seattle law firm. I never received a response.

Those early months set the stage for my ultimate failure in law. I'll never know how much of this failure was nature or nurture. Today, I feel so bad for that young woman who assumed that everything would be fair, who assumed that everything would play out as it should. That young woman didn't have the self-confidence to approach a kindly partner (though I'm not sure if I could have even found one) and explicitly ask to be mentored. Had someone agreed, might I have been able to turn the ship around? Given that the most sinister events at Schiffer Mulligan were still yet to come, I'm guessing the answer is no.

Outside of work, the large Chestnut Street apartment that I was supposed to share with Mike slowly became *my* home. In a way, it was a blessing that he never moved in because that apartment was untarnished by memories of him being there. The one-bedroom was old-time-y San Francisco, with a black-and-white tile floor in the bathroom and a mint green sink and tub. I loved the old hardwood floors, the huge living room and even the minimalist in me loved the surplus of closet space. It was at once spacious and cozy. I loved hearing the nearby fog horn — signaling land to ships crossing under the Golden Gate Bridge — when Mensch and I slept in on weekend mornings.

Feeling isolated and lonely at the firm, I was as attached to Mensch as a pet owner could be. To Mensch, I wasn't the "crazy ex-girlfriend" or "the unproductive associate." He was a constant — always available for affection, always eager to be with me. His name took on a kind of irony because I met a grand total of zero mensches — men of integrity with a strong sense of right and wrong — in Big Law.

After three years in Los Angeles, where the traffic — along with the post-Rodney King-verdict riots — enervated me by the end of my time there, I rejoiced living in San Francisco. Compared to the strip malls of L.A., the city's charming neighborhoods and distinct micro-climates appealed to me. The Marina District was a hub for 20-somethings, complete with Noah's Bagels, dive bars, World Wrapps, and take-out Mexican food. Most of all, I loved that everything I needed — from a movie theater to a pharmacy to a neighborhood grocery store to a post office — was all within eight blocks. In strict contrast to my life in L.A., I rarely used my car other than to drive to work. Oddly, it was that year at Schiffer Mulligan that I developed road rage, something I hadn't experienced even when I lived in over-congested Los Angeles. Perhaps I associated the act of driving itself with transport to a place I loathed. Road rage was the outlet for the anger I couldn't express at work.

Despite my shrunken sense of self, I managed to maintain a limited social life, including rollerblading with college friends. I also became friends with Reggie and Irv, two other junior associates at Schiffer Mulligan who were far outside The Club as they had joined the firm not from the summer associate program but when their environmental law group had "lateraled" to Schiffer from another firm. We had lunches together and went downstairs for afternoon coffee. We saw movies on the weekends and often went to author readings at bookstores.

I did have one of the best weekends of my life during that soul-crushing year, though by most peoples' measure it might not rank high. It poured rain from Friday afternoon through Monday morning. I'd recently purchased some books by Anne Lamott and Raymond Carver. It was a rare weekend when I had no social plans. I had nowhere to go. For the entire 48 hours, I sat in bed with Mensch purring at my side, reading book after book, getting out of bed only to use the bathroom or order a burrito to be delivered, all with the cozy sound of rain falling outside. I was alone, doing what I loved, with no outside demands. It was a rare period of peace during that year.

Rising to my alarm clock Monday morning to return to Schiffer Mulligan and navigate The Club and my pitiful billable hours was almost physically painful.

Chapter Seven

1994

By the late spring of 1994, I went from sad and confused about the breakup and frustrated by my lack of projects to increasingly afraid to go to work. Mike's actions had gone from hurtful and insensitive to explicitly cruel. Every morning I had to summon outsized measures of emotional reserves to get ready, to outwardly disguise the way I felt inside, to present myself as a capable professional. Because inside, I was a wreck.

According to my notes in The File, one day Mike left me a long and chiding voicemail, the substance of which I don't remember. Shortly thereafter, I received a knock on my office door and Mike entered.

"I have not done anything to ruin your career at Schiffer," he said, among other things. "But believe me, I could."

I took this statement for the threat that it was, so distraught that I left the office and did not return for two days. The trapped and lonely feeling was laced with indignant flashes of disbelief.

In what world was someone who behaved like this beloved *by the firm?*

And I couldn't get anyone of import to understand. When I later told Ben that Mike had threatened me, he responded, "I don't doubt it." But nothing changed — for me or for Mike.

Walking into work, roaming the halls on my way to the library, waiting by the elevator, I'd smile at partners and associates, always wondering what untruth they'd heard about me.

Were they part of the discussion comparing me in bed with the firm librarian Mike had slept with?

Did they hear that I had the lowest billable hours of any litigator and did they think that was because of my abilities?

Were they on their way to a social event — firm-sponsored or otherwise — that I wasn't invited to?

Mike also brought a new girlfriend to the office and firm events. Although by this time, I no longer hoped that Mike would change his mind about me, his parading her around was awful in its own way. I wondered what kind of conversations her presence sparked in The Club.

Oh, she's way *cuter than Erin.*

Way to level up, dBaum.

These conversations may or may not have happened but I couldn't help speculating about them. His bringing her to our mutual workplace — a completely optional maneuver on his part — left me hurt and embarrassed. As Jennifer Aniston once said about Brad Pitt, I felt there was "a sensitivity chip that's missing" in Mike.

In The File, I found parts of an email exchange between me and Mike dated May 9, 1994. I don't remember what triggered this exchange, but it seemed to be about me requesting to receive work assignments directly from partners, not from Mike himself, who was only a year ahead of me in seniority. I checked in with modern-day law firm lawyers who confirmed that it was and remains highly unusual for a second-year associate to give assignments to a first-year associate. Given how little work I was given from anyone at the firm, Mike wanting to give me an assignment was, I suspect, a power play.

Mike wrote:

"[W]e are the two lowest-level litigators in our commercial litigation department at this time. Inevitably, if I need help with a project, I am advised to turn to you. I have tried to handle this situation in a professional manner, and in a number of cases I have taken projects that I would otherwise assign [to you] to avoid a difficult situation. In short, I resort to you only when necessary. If you do not feel you can adequately perform an assignment from me on these rare occasions (in this case, 'adequately' means the same job you would do for somebody else — I'll assume that your work is usually better than the work you did on this case today), then I am more than willing to tell the partner that I am working with (whomever that may be) that you insist on speaking with him or her directly for personal reasons. I don't believe this approach will reflect well on you nor do I believe most of our partners will enjoy spending their time on a matter they would otherwise delegate to a second-year associate. I suggest you think it over."

I replied, telling him that after everything I'd put up with in the previous seven months, it was too much to ask that I sit across from him with a pad and paper writing down everything he said. It was not lost on me that I was being lectured on "professional" behavior from someone who had a lurid past at the firm, including sleeping with multiple employees (me and the librarian, being the two I knew about) and over-drinking at firm events. He was using his insider status to isolate me and prey on my insecurity.

In what should have been good news, Mike announced on June 16, 1994 that he was leaving Schiffer Mulligan for a new job at a Silicon Valley firm. Spiteful as ever, though, he couldn't help sending me an email threatening the job prospects of Kat, a female summer associate who was my official "mentee." An email exchange from that day is in The File. I don't know the context of this exchange but it illustrates that a conversation that should have been professional devolved into nastiness.

Mike wrote:

"I think you should consider how your actions will affect others before you take an action like Tuesday's. I am on this office's recruiting committee and I think you should have considered Kat's job prospects when you divulged that she reported my actions to you. I would be less likely to recommend giving her an offer based on this incident not because of a personal vendetta, but because I generally think people should mind their own business. I don't think it is very thoughtful of you to drag others along with you. Feel free to pass this along to Kat."

When I replied, taking exception to his erroneous presumptions about a conversation between me and Kat, he responded only to point out two typos in my message: "Perceived is spelled with an ei, and there is only one r in harassment. Good try, though."

Not knowing that Mike had given notice, I printed the emails and brought them to Ben's office to show him what I'd been dealing with for so many months, to show that Mike was now threatening *a summer associate's* career. I will never forget the look on Ben's face. It was unadulterated disinterest and annoyance — with *me*. I left his office feeling as small as I've ever felt. Not only did partners and associates talk about my private life and fail to properly manage my hours, they stood by and *let* Mike treat me (and now a female summer associate) poorly. When I raised the problem, nothing changed.

The firm threw him a huge going-away party at Splendido's, a fancy restaurant in the Embarcadero. I'd always tried to let his behavior and questionable judgment speak for itself but absolutely nothing he did affected the firm's attitude towards him. Mike had been at the firm first and one year longer and had some pre-established relationships that caused attorneys to take sides. But that I was not treated with equal deference — having done nothing worse than falling in love and having my heart broken — can only be attributable to my gender.

A few weeks before Mike gave notice, I'd declined to attend the upcoming summer associate event in Lake Tahoe, even though I was a summer associate mentor to Kat. After my simple "no," Tim Reids (the same senior associate who said the applicant with a misspelling on his resume was excused because he was a "very handsome guy") pressured me to explain why I wasn't going. I did not say that I was busy or had a conflict. Instead, I honestly replied that I did not want to be around Mike for an entire weekend. Shockingly, after Mike gave notice, the feeling was not, "Oh, great, now Erin, who is a summer associate mentor and actually *works* at the firm can now go." Instead, Tim arranged for Mike to attend the Tahoe weekend — on the firm's dime — even though by then *he hadn't worked at the firm for two weeks*.

Similarly, even though I explicitly told Ben about threats and that I was afraid of Mike, Ben still invited Mike to the end-of-summer party — at Ben's house — *after* Mike left the firm.

I felt trapped. I was still in my first year so I couldn't quit. I had already spoken to Ben several times over the months trying to get him to understand what I was dealing with. But nothing changed. I feared that if I complained more, I'd soon be out of a job. I knew what was taking place at the firm was wrong, but I feared retaliation from Schiffer Mulligan itself or, were I to leave noisily, in the San Francisco legal community. I had trouble concentrating. One night I sank down onto my kitchen floor crying hysterically, doing the only thing I could think to do — call my aunt, a therapist, who first confirmed that I was not suicidal before talking me down. I would soon understand that the targeted poor treatment I experienced at Schiffer Mulligan was textbook hostile work environment harassment, which destabilizes an employee's mental health and quality of life. And the definitive moments were still yet to come.

***

On July 22, 1994, without being consulted, I was reassigned from the litigation department to the busier labor and employment department. I still hadn't received my six-month review, even though I started at the firm in October and had been asking Elizabeth, the partner in charge of reviews, for it ever since the six-month mark. Part of the problem was the partners didn't even give me enough work to properly evaluate my capabilities and the bulk of projects I was given were last-minute one-offs.

The last straw, the smoking gun, occurred on July 23. A secretary I was friendly with (since I actually interacted with staff in the break room), came into my office and solemnly shut the door.

"What's going on?" I asked.

She silently handed me a file folder with a single white sheet inside. "I found this on the printer." These were the days when most communications were printed and multiple secretaries shared a single printer.

"Is it bad?" I asked. Yet I already knew.

She pursed her lips together and nodded.

The *full* text of the Jasper Brook memo:

July 23, 1994

To Frederick Duncan

From: Jasper Brook

This will confirm that I did not agree to this "reassignment." I agreed that I would take primary responsibility for keeping Erin busy until reviews have taken place and a "keep/not keep" decision was made thereafter. However, since you have unilaterally announced the "reassignment" to the entire office, I will go along. Don't ever do it again. The labor department is my responsibility. You do not "decide" to reassign anyone to the labor department. The fact that you consulted with Doug Easter is not sufficient.

As I noted in the meeting, Ms. Gordon is the least productive associate in the litigation group. The response to her work has been mixed, at best. I suspect that she will become, if not already, a problem associate. Her "interpersonal skills" have been placed in question by her interaction with Davenbaum — she "Marvin'd" him after they broke off a relationship by forcing him to pay 1/2 of her rent. This caused tension in the office which, I am told, hastened Mike's departure. It also signals a judgment problem. The one memo she prepared for me was mediocre, and displayed weak analytical skills and no depth whatsoever. You and I have both written off considerable amounts of her time on [client] matters. From all indications she is an attorney who is about to be identified as one who is not going to make it. Her review is past due, and it was my determination that until that was done, no "reassignment" should [sic] effectuated. I agreed only that I would load her up to give her an opportunity to show that she at least had the willingness to work if given some to do. If her hours remained low, she would have no excuse. By the reassignment, and the assurances of Erin's strengths which accompanied it, we now must give her a "fresh start" meaning we must start all over again to document our dissatisfaction, after, of course, we give her labor/employment law training, mentoring, counselling [sic] and every opportunity to show that she cannot do the job, or that she can. The labor department leverage ratio of 4 associates per partner demonstrates that we have little time to devote to this personnel issue, and certainly will not be able to make a speedy or efficient decision, or spend a lot of time building a record for termination. If she is not a "keeper" this reassignment has cost the firm a lot of money in her continued salary and benefits. What is done is done. I will move her up to the labor wing, and will see to it that she attends the requisite seminars, gets a heavy work-load, and gets her hours up. I just hope that [you do] not see this as Schiffer's answer to a downturn in general litigation.

The secretary left my office and moments later Reggie, one of my few friends at the firm, happened to pop in. He observed me shaking uncontrollably. I handed him the memo. Reggie explained that the "Marvin'd" comment referred to actor Lee Marvin, who was sued by his former lover in the 1970's, resulting in the establishment of the right of partners in non-married relationships to sue for a division of property.

I know that *I* had never spoken to Jasper Brook about my relationship, which proved that my personal life was a topic of discussion among partners. Whether from years of zealously litigating or a desire to protect the institution, the leaders of the firm were completely desensitized to me as a person.

Not only was the memo nasty and unequivocally confirmed that partners had been discussing my private life and making decisions based on it, the memo was also littered with inaccuracies.

The inherent sexism in the "palimony" reference was shocking enough, particularly because it could in no way be relevant to my work performance. But it was also *wrong*. The payments were for a short time, not "half the rent," and were solely Mike's idea.

Also wrong: I did not hasten Mike's departure. He'd been looking to leave Schiffer Mulligan long before I even started there. He even applied to business school that fall (which he didn't end up attending) and had interviewed at other firms. (Years later, he published an essay about why he never wanted his mother to visit his first law office because he hated being a Schiffer lawyer; in the piece he also managed to publicly disparage his mother.)

The day before the Brook memo, when I'd been reassigned to the labor department, litigator Don Wu insisted that I stay on his case in the litigation department. If I was that bad of a lawyer, wouldn't he have been delighted to take me off the case?

Jasper Brook's memo absolutely wrecked me. I had never felt so hopeless and frustrated. I'd lost a shocking 17 pounds that year because of stress. I couldn't prove my competence with work because I didn't have any. I wasn't learning or developing as an attorney. I was wholly iced out of The Club, which clearly had sway in the power structure. I did not know how to get people to understand what had *really* happened — that the rapid acceleration of our relationship had all been Mike's idea, that he turned on me on a dime at the worst, most heartless time possible. Other than a couple of other low-level associates, I had no one on my side. I was pleading with people committed to misunderstanding me. I felt so alone and unseen. It was crazy making. Recently, in 2022, someone I know took a paid leave of absence from work for emotional distress *caused* by work. To paraphrase King George in the musical "Hamilton," I wasn't aware that was something a person could do. There's no question I would have qualified that year.

Instead, I went to work utterly bewildered that this kind of career sabotage was happening to me. I realize now that this is a measure of my privilege. I was raised by white, upper middle-class parents who were often "fixers" of my problems. In the fitness industry, there's the concept of "time under tension," meaning that the more stress you put your muscles under, the more likely they are to adapt, consequently building strength. When I joined Schiffer Mulligan, many of my problems had been "fixed" by adults so I had little experience dealing with hardship. I was suddenly facing a significant challenge my parents could not fix. I had no past triumphs over hardship from which I could draw strength. (All of this later informed my own parenting. When my daughter was dealing with an arrogant and rude boss while working at a coffee shop during high school, I encouraged her to look him in the eye and insist that he couldn't yell at her in front of customers. "If he fires you for standing up," I told her, "who cares?" I wanted her to have practice, at 17, standing up for herself in a low-stakes situation. She did, and her boss stopped speaking to her disrespectfully.)

I have little patience for self-pitying individuals who constantly complain about things that happen *to* them, people who don't take ownership of their part in a problem. In re-examining my 1993-1994 from a 2023 lens, I'm mindful of taking responsibility. I don't want to be criticized for blaming others, particularly when I actually spent the last 30 years blaming *myself*.

What I own:

I did not know myself at age 25. I didn't realize early enough that I lacked the killer instinct that a good litigator needs, that I was not constitutionally suited to the hierarchical structure and demands of a big, cut-throat law firm with high-stakes cases.

I should have been more proactive about exploring different practice areas. My husband is a commercial real estate attorney who helps clients buy and sell properties and assists developers in building new projects. Until I met him, I had little knowledge of that kind of transactional law practice. I look back and wonder what choices I'd have made if I'd had broader exposure to less combative law practices. Real estate law, adoption law...

I cared too much and probably tried too hard to be accepted by the "in" crowd.

I once referred to Mike as "my ex" in a handwritten note to partner Elizabeth (more on her soon) RSVP'ing to a firm-sponsored party at her house. That one, small reference meant that Dixon Long (more on him soon too) could snap nastily at me — as if I were a hostile witness on the stand in court — when I told him I never spoke to partners about my relationship.

I own that I once hooked up (though didn't sleep with) with a senior associate at Schiffer Mulligan. It was towards the end of my tenure there, after Mike had left. I was lonely and horny. He was tall, decent looking and a nice enough guy, but overall, a complete doofus with a borderline social disorder, the kind where he didn't understand when to stop talking in order to have a normal back-and-forth conversation. He was the kind of guy who'd talk *at* you. I'd heard members of The Club (of which he was a very, very peripheral member) making fun of him behind his back. We ended up bonding over the fact that he, too, had been duped by a romantic partner. In his case, he went to his girlfriend's apartment to surprise her and discovered that she shared that apartment with a live-in boyfriend. We talked at length about the pain of feeling so connected to someone only to have that connection abruptly severed and being left wondering if it had ever even been real. At some point after our encounter (again, not sex), he said we shouldn't move forward. When he saw that I was upset, he got mad and said, referring to my Mike-related heartbreak of the last many months, "What? Is it that anyone who doesn't love you is evil?" I didn't want to tell him that what I was really upset about was the fact that I couldn't believe I was being shut down by someone like him, someone I didn't even really *like*.

I own that, in an immature move motivated by lingering pain, in 1997 I mailed an anonymous note to Mike suggesting he read the book *Animal Husbandry* by Laura

Zigman. The novel's premise, according to the Amazon description: "Ray makes the move. Jane feels the rush. Ray says the L-word. Jane breaks her lease. Then suddenly, inexplicably, he dumps her. Just. Like. That."

Chapter Eight

1994

During and long after that year, bizarrely I wished that something more...explicit had happened. Because even back then, people understood that quid pro quo sexual harassment — the "give me a blow job or I'll make sure you never make partner" behavior — is unequivocally wrong. Quid pro quo translates to "this for that" and refers to managers or supervisors directly or indirectly demanding sexual favors in exchange for a workplace benefit or to avoid termination or demotion.

After the Jasper Brook memo, when I told one of my best friends from law school that I was considering consulting an employment lawyer about a hostile work environment claim, she asked, with a distinct note of skepticism, "What, someone said you had to have sex — or else?" Those conversations where I had to explain, to provide definitions, to give examples — even to other lawyers, even to people who loved me — chipped more deeply away at my self-esteem and my resolve. A voice in my head insisted that I was simply weak, that I should just suck it all up, that "maybe it really wasn't that bad." Years of conditioning and gaslighting will do that. It's like the difference between a physically abusive parent and one who, over time, diminishes a child's self-worth or is emotionally unavailable.

I endured many, many episodes that on their own might seem minor or insignificant. But their cumulative effect over many months, orchestrated by several different lawyers at the firm, were devastating not just to my confidence but to my career. The Jasper Brook memo was undoubtedly the culmination of — and the smoking gun showing — the long pattern of abuse. But the incident that unquestionably *hurt* the most was seeing my photo defaced by someone at the firm.

Background: I spent a fair amount of time that year hunkering down in my apartment, recovering from emotionally challenging work weeks by re-watching "Desperately Seeking Susan," my comfort movie then, on VHS tape. But 1993 was also the year I started taking writing classes at night and on the weekends. I'd always been a voracious reader — my Judy Blume books fell apart because I re-read them so many times as a child. With no work to do despite my repeated efforts to pitch in on any case in any way, the hours spent in my office reading were both humiliating and strangely enriching. In addition to Raymond Carver short stories and James Herriot books about his work as a veterinarian in Yorkshire England, I was also obsessed with the first-person essays by *San Francisco Chronicle* columnist Adair Lara, one of the professional writers with whom I took classes.

To use modern parlance, I vibed immediately with first-person, personal essays like Lara's. I wrote a lot about being a new lawyer and everything I sent out (and those were the days of actually printing out an essay on a dot-matrix printer and sending it out to an editor by snail mail) was getting published.

I wrote about living in San Francisco, about being a young adult, about what I'd do if I won the lottery. One piece I wrote about being a new lawyer ran, along with my photo, in *The Recorder*, one of San Francisco's two legal newspapers. My sweet secretary, who was proud of the accomplishment, photocopied it and taped it up in the copy room. One day I walked in to discover that someone had drawn devil horns and a mustache on my face.

I stopped cold in my tracks. I felt all of the blood in my body pool in my chest cavity. I lost my breath from shock and confusion. It was like I'd been gut-punched. I hadn't felt that belittled since...perhaps ever, but certainly not since elementary school.

I tore it down and dashed to my office where I shut the door, tears burning my eyes. I was already feeling so vulnerable, and this confirmed that I continued to be a target of teasing and ridicule among my fellow lawyers.

When I opened The File in 2023, I found USPS letters from people I didn't know who'd written to me after that very essay with my photo had been published. A sampling:

May 6, 1994

"The attitude that you expressed in your commentary tells me that you will be a leader in the firm of your choice."

Undated, handwritten

"Your intriguing and humble perspective already separates you from many of your peers."

June 6, 1994

"Congratulations on your very nice article in *The Recorder*. I found it quite moving. In spite of the bad press we lawyers get, I am amazed to see how many really fine people there are practicing law. You, for one....You've demonstrated by your sensitive essay your real worth as a human being."

Undated, handwritten

"[T]hanks for taking time to remind me how proud I am of what I've accomplished, and how proud all attorneys should be. Keep writing. I think you've got a knack for it!"

June 14, 1994

"Just wanted you to know that there's another SF attorney out there who thoroughly enjoyed your 'Perspective' article, thought it was exceptionally well-written, and has faithfully carried it around in his briefcase since the day it was published!"

Side note about writing... Back when Mike and I were dating, before I'd graduated from law school or taken my first writing class, Mike had told me *he* was interested in writing. It was the heyday of Seinfeld, when observational humor was hot, the kind of humor at which Mike excelled and to which he aspired. He told me once that he'd spent an entire weekend afternoon writing a funny essay and then somehow his computer deleted it. (Again, this was long before the Cloud.) Free time was at a premium then when he was a first-year lawyer, and he was *so* aggravated that he'd spent hours of precious weekend time on something and ended up with nothing to show for it. Looking back, I see that — whether it was Mike who defaced my photo or someone else — he may have been jealous of my being published. That's maybe why Mike, in his glee in reporting anyone's negative thoughts about me, told me The Club made fun of me for framing and hanging in my office my first couple of published essays. Women, I've come to understand, are not supposed to be proud of or, worse, parade their accomplishments. Bragging or appearing self-promotional "feels dirtier than the floor of a football stadium after a three-hour show," wrote Emily Halnon in a CNN opinion piece about Taylor Swift's unabashed pride in being the first woman to sell out arenas all over the US.

According to the US Equal Employment Opportunity Commission, harassment — a form of employment discrimination — is unwelcome conduct based on race, color, religion, sex (including sexual orientation, gender identity, or pregnancy), national origin, older age, disability or genetic information. It includes conduct that is severe or pervasive enough to create a work environment *that a reasonable person would consider intimidating, hostile, or abusive.* Petty slights, annoyances, and isolated non-serious incidents become unlawful when the conduct creates a work environment that would be *intimi-*

dating, hostile, or offensive to reasonable people. Offensive conduct may include offensive jokes, slurs, epithets or name calling, physical assaults or *threats, intimidation, ridicule or mockery, insults or put-downs, offensive objects or pictures,* and interference with work performance.

Fucking textbook.

Workplace bullying is a newer — and related — concept. Examples include *deliberate exclusion of individuals from meetings or activities they should be attending; shunning, excluding, marginalizing; personal attacks or threatening comments; setting someone up to fail; gossip mongering or rumor spreading; and telling personal jokes about a coworker.* According to labor and employment expert Patricia Gillette, workplace bullying in law firms is subtle and can take the form of not getting the same kind of work as colleagues. "It's much more personal because it's mean and it goes to your core," Gillette said. "It often goes unnoticed and unreported because it's harder to define."

According to a 2021 *Psychology Today* article, workplace bullies may have high levels of narcissism or psychopathy that lead them to manipulate or belittle others for personal gain. Workplace bullying is a kind of "degradation ceremony," which punishes the victim while strengthening bonds between other in-group members. Mike instrumentalized our failed relationship — to raise himself up and to keep me down. Complicity is part of the culture in which money and power trump morality, leaving a trail of devastation and pain, according to the article.

In contrast to using power to demand sexual favors, hostile work environment harassment and workplace bullying are more ambiguous, subtle and subjective. But it's still an actionable form of harassment, particularly if the employer knows about the environment and does nothing about it. Experts agree that hostile environment harassment includes crude talk about a coworker's body and discussing sexual experiences with coworkers. Some experts, including Beth Richie, a professor of Criminology, Law and Justice at the University of Illinois at Chicago, characterize harassment as a form of gender violence.

Gender violence.

Reading that sucked the air out of my lungs.

If you haven't seen the 2010 movie "Trust," I can't recommend it enough for educational purposes. It centers on 14-year-old Annie, who has become friends with Charlie, a 16-year-old boy she meets in a teen Internet chat room. As they become closer, he reveals to Annie that he's actually 20. When they decide, after months of grooming by Charlie, to secretly meet in person, Annie discovers that her "boyfriend" is really a 35-year-old man. He takes her to a motel where he rapes her. Still, Annie believes that Charlie truly loves her and, when her parents and the authorities find out what happened, Annie insists that everyone is overreacting. But when law enforcement shows Annie photos of other teen girls that Charlie raped, Annie runs to her therapist, played by Viola Davis. In an incredible scene, viewers witness the precise moment that Annie finally grasps that she wasn't in a relationship at all but, in fact, had been raped.

I have not been raped and am in no way suggesting that what happened at Schiffer Mulligan was as abhorrent as what happened to Annie and anyone who has been raped. But that scene shows the power of realization dawning. Applying *the language of trauma* to an event changes the way we process it, according to "The Resilience Gap," a 2023 article in *The Atlantic*. Therefore, if you want to know what it was like for me to read that a hostile work environment and workplace bullying are forms of gender violence, what it was like for me to read the definition of "gaslighting" and in a millisecond grasp that *that* is exactly why my year at Schiffer Mulligan affected me so deeply and for so long, watch the scene from "Trust," watch the power of Annie's realization.

To me, the events at Schiffer Mulligan — from the Brook memo to the defacement of my photo to being excluded from firm-sponsored social events I had every right to attend — were related to my gender. As far as I'm aware, no one was writing memos about the inappropriateness of the *men* at the firm discussing my sex life. *Mike's* "interpersonal" skills were not called into question even though he apparently spent the summer before I joined the firm badmouthing me and had physical relationships with women at the firm, which he bragged about to others.

Some might argue that I was too sensitive, that my skin wasn't thick enough, that my privileged upbringing meant that I lacked the necessary emotional tools to handle what happened that year. To this, I say *I agree*. But in law, there's an important concept known as the "eggshell plaintiff" doctrine. It means that a defendant takes the victim as he or she finds the victim, even a victim who's as fragile and delicate as an eggshell. By law, a defendant cannot escape liability simply because a plaintiff might be more susceptible to injury than other people. A defendant is responsible for all injuries, whether the victim is sturdy and heals rapidly or if the victim, for whatever reasons, is more likely to suffer injury.

In other words, emotional damage — like "lived experience" — is personal. No one can tell you that what you've experienced is not traumatic. The same experiences can affect people differently. Experts are in 100 percent agreement that trauma can be triggered by events that make one feel *humiliated, rejected, invalidated, unsupported, trapped, ashamed and powerless*. Given how many hours people spend at work, a toxic workplace can profoundly harm an employee's mental health, triggering anxiety, depression, and can even damage physical health.

Having my photo defaced by some unknown colleague, hung on the wall of the copy room for all to see, deprived me of my humanity. I wasn't seen as a person, let alone a colleague. The effects of this workplace mistreatment didn't end when my time at Schiffer Mulligan came to an end. To the contrary, it reverberated through my life, changing its trajectory altogether.

Chapter Nine

1994

A day after consulting with Lynn, a family friend who was an employment lawyer, about how to respond to Jasper Brook's highly inappropriate memo about my personal life, I approached the office of Frederick Duncan, the San Francisco office's managing partner. I found in The File the exact sheet I held in my hand that day. It — and I — said:

"The comments about Mike are highly inappropriate, irrelevant and most importantly, incorrect. I object to words like 'Marvin'd' and I am shocked that my personal life would be brought up among the partners. Not only are these comments in poor judgment but they are riddled with inaccuracies.

[Regarding the rent Mike contributed to:] As far as I'm concerned this was a private issue and should not be considered by anyone here in decisions regarding my career.

[Regarding my "hastening" Mike's departure:] Mike interviewed at another firm in the summer of 1993 and applied to business school last fall, both of which took place before I even got here.

I have also been subjected to threats to 'ruin my career' and other unfair treatment to which I put the firm on notice by speaking about it to a partner numerous times and it continued nonetheless through Mike's departure. I object to being termed a 'problem' associate — I always felt my issues with Mike were private; yet he consistently discussed our issues throughout the firm.

Despite these threats and other adversity, as a first-year, I singlehandedly set up a meeting with the president of [a large construction company] and [a senior construction law partner]. I am disappointed that, after showing my commitment to this firm in the face of hostility, I am not treated with equal respect.

I am concerned about this email because it sounds as if I'm going to be set up to fail in the labor department.

I have a right to expect reasonable projects and a reasonable workload.

If I decide to leave the firm as a result of this unfair treatment, I believe that on the basis of what's happened that I can expect to be adequately compensated, to receive reasonable continuation of health benefits and appropriate recommendations.

I want an acknowledgment that this was improper, irrelevant and untrue and I don't want this in my file."

I finished in tears, apologizing for my emotion, which diluted the strength of my message. I was trembling and felt sick, terrified that I'd just torpedoed my fledgling career.

Before that day, my interactions with Frederick Duncan were minimal, though the very day before the Brook memo was written, Frederick came into my office (by this time, many months into my first year, I'd been moved upstairs in a symbolic but ineffective effort to integrate me into the firm) to personally deliver my version of a memo that other "underproductive" associates received.

"As of June 30, 1994, your billable hours were 580.4. In order to meet the 1900 hour billable requirement for the year, you will need to sustain a 219.9 hour per month pace for the balance of the year. Please see me if you have any questions about attaining this goal."

Though every litigation associate received their own version this memo, I was (as Brook's memo pointed out) the litigation department's least productive associate, which made sense given that I was also the most junior. Frederick chastised me in my office that day much like a disappointed father. I responded to him by opening a drawer and pulling out my stack of emails and handwritten notes, detailing every single time I had let partners and senior associates know that I needed projects to work on. It was nearly an inch thick. But Frederick was unmoved as I flipped through the pages with my thumb.

That very paper trail was a large part of The File. My notes began as early as my fifth week at the firm, in early November 1993. There were several printed emails like this one from December: "Hi Ben! I'm going to be sworn into the federal bar on Tuesday 10 a.m. I'll be in the office after it's over and desperately in need of work. Just thought I'd let you know since I haven't been assigned to anyone yet. Thanks!"

Another: "Kristy Potts told me that you're taking over the case involving East Virginia Bank. I did a tiny research project for her on that case so if you need any help on the case once she leaves, let me know."

In addition to the printed emails, my handwritten notes detailed no fewer than 19 phone calls and voicemails, mostly to Ben, all the way through June. My notations included words like, "Asked Kimberly G. if she needed follow up work done on earlier project" and "Emailed Powell & Tim R. re: Best Buy & Macy's matters."

How was I supposed to bill 220 hours a month when no one would give me work? I was being scolded for something over which I, a first-year, had zero control.

In Frederick's office that day, I told him that, contrary to Brook's memo, it wasn't true that "from all indications [I am] an attorney who is about to be identified as one who is not going to make it." After asking for my six-month performance review for months, I finally got it around the 10-month mark. I wasn't allowed to make photocopies of the written reviews — looking back, I wonder if other associates had been allowed to — but I did take notes until Elizabeth, who was the partner in charge of the reviews and responsible for the inexcusable delay, practically kicked me out of her office because she had "somewhere to be."

In those days, Schiffer Mulligan associates were evaluated on paper forms using a 1-5 scale, with 5 being the best.

Don Wu, the partner I'd done the most substantive work for, gave me all 4's in the legal skills category and a 4.5 for clarity of writing.

Senior associate Trina Young gave me all 4's.

Kimberly gave me 5's for written product and legal reasoning. She also described me as "eager, pleasant, an asset to the firm."

Labor partner Doug Easter gave me mostly 4's, noting that I "could improve on juggling a number of projects, like all new attorneys."

Mid-level associate Kristy Potts wrote, "Follows through, asks questions."

Ben wrote "[Erin] identifies business opportunities," and noted that diligence was my "strong suit" and that one client I worked with directly responded by sending the firm two new matters.

These positive remarks included evaluations from several attorneys who left the firm months before the Brook memo so I know that they were not "padded" to lighten the blow or appease me after the Brook memo. And notably, after my "reassignment" from the litigation to the labor group, litigation partner Don Wu explicitly told me in a voicemail (that my secretary transcribed and is in The File) that he wanted me to remain on the case I'd been working on with him. He also said, quite indelicately, that it was up to me to manage any conflicts with new labor department assignments, "including coming in nights and weekends if you have to."

After I cried in Frederick's office, my interactions with him and other leadership at the firm focused on my assertion — supported by specific examples — that I was in a hostile work environment. I immediately felt, as Frances Conley described in her memoir about sexism at Stanford Medical School, *Walking Out on the Boys*, the "force of institutional strength."

Days later, in early August, the firm sent Dixon Long, a labor partner from another office, to San Francisco to investigate my claim of a hostile work environment. When he came to my office to discuss what I'd experienced during the previous 10 months, his tone was accusatory, nasty, dismissive and skeptical. With a sneer, he questioned me as if I were a hostile witness, rather than an attorney raising serious concerns, backed with written evidence, about a hostile work environment at the firm in which he was a co-owner. His investigation was undoubtedly partial. Later that same day, I saw him get in the elevator to have lunch with none other than...Jasper Brook, the partner who'd written the memo at the center of it all.

When Dixon Long returned to my office after completing his "investigation," he informed me that I had not, in fact, experienced a hostile work environment but, according to my handwritten notes, he conceded that "something was going on."

Not one person claimed the events I described hadn't happened.

The firm was sorry I saw the memo. (Read: sorry it got caught.) As far as I was aware, there were zero consequences for Jasper Brook, a labor lawyer no less.

The singular change that Schiffer Mulligan leadership made after my internal claim was to institute a mandatory arbitration agreement for all associates and staff going forward.

A memo dated August 25, 1994, just days after the Dixon Long investigation, sent to all attorneys, read:

"The entering Class of 1994 associates, and lateral attorneys and staff hired after September 1, 1994, will be required to sign an arbitration agreement prior to commencing their employment with the Firm."

This agreement provides, in part, that, "any controversy or claim arising out of my employment with Schiffer, Mulligan, Hamlin & Raptor ('the Firm'), or the termination of the employment relationship, including any claim based in whole or in part on federal, state or local laws, whether statutory or common law, shall be settled and resolved by arbitration." These kinds of mandatory arbitration agreements are considered "contracts of adhesion," meaning that the signing party has no opportunity to negotiate its terms. And today, mandatory arbitration agreements like these are largely prohibited in employment settings.

Coming directly on the heels of Dixon Long's investigation, this firm-wide change in policy shows what I'd set in motion. The partners were afraid. The new policy showed they were deliberately seeking to silence voices — current, like mine, or future — that objected to or highlighted inappropriate behavior taking place there.

Other than the establishment of this draconian new policy, nothing changed. I was furious and panicked. My options were to stay at the firm where I was considered a pariah; quit and be unemployed; try to find a new job barely one year out of law school, which was highly unusual in those days; or sue.

I was made to feel that *I* was the one with the problem, that I was too sensitive, even vindictive. My feelings and experiences were trivialized. And that made me feel whiny and bothersome. I couldn't understand — and still don't — what *I* had done that was so terrible.

This, I understand only now, was textbook *institutional* gaslighting, which occurs at an organizational level. The online Urban Dictionary, of all sources, has a surprisingly cogent description of this phenomenon:

"When a group of respected people within an institution are posed as investigating on the victim's behalf, but in actuality act to belittle or deny the reality of the harm committed in order to protect the institution's reputation, the institution can cause the victim to question their own perceptions of reality, feelings, instincts, and even sanity.... When an institution gaslights a victim in order to protect its own reputation, the institutional betrayal silences, invalidates, and harms recent survivors in their most vulnerable states."

Soon after Dixon Long's sham investigation, I learned that the few friends I had at the firm were discreetly told to disassociate themselves from me for "political" reasons. I also learned that one secretary was, inexplicably, telling other staff members that I had "caused a lot of problems for the firm."

A compassionate, sincere apology, combined with appropriate repercussions for Jasper Brook and certain members of The Club, would have gone a long, long way towards restoring my emotional equilibrium and maybe even would have gotten my career on track. Simple validation that the behavior I encountered was intolerable would have helped me recalibrate and move on. Apparently I'm not alone. I found in The File an October 1994 *American Lawyer* article titled "Does Being a Lawyer Mean Never Having to Say You're Sorry?" The article reported that most victims of harassment simply "want you to validate their feelings, and to stop it from happening....Most victims of racial and sexual discrimination just want an acknowledgment or an apology."

But the firm conceded nothing, gave not one inch.

I stood up for myself. I screamed from the rooftops and no one listened. It showed how impossible my situation at Schiffer Mulligan was. That's when I finally decided to seek my own legal counsel.

Chapter Ten

1994

Schiffer Mulligan's Firm Policies and Procedures, tucked into The File, read, in part, "We encourage any person who believes that harassment or other discrimination is occurring to report the conduct to any member of the Diversity Committee or Executive Committee, or to the Administrative Partner, Office Manager or Personnel Manager." Sexual harassment was defined in the policies as, "Such conduct [that] has the purpose or effect of unreasonably interfering with the individual's work performance, or creating an intimidating, hostile, offensive or abusive working environment." Conduct may include: "Uninvited discussion of sexual experiences, desires, values or concerns." Any report will be treated confidentially and with trained impartial attorneys, according to the policies, and the firm also claimed to have a non-retaliation policy.

Dixon Long had proved himself to be the furthest thing from an impartial attorney, and I *was* being retaliated against for objecting to the Jasper Brook memo and other (likely illegal) treatment I'd experienced. The grand result of the Long "investigation" was — wait for it — that I would get the privilege of continuing to work at Schiffer Mulligan.

I then spoke to two plaintiff-side employment lawyers, both highly recommended by family friends. One was Cliff Palefsky. My handwritten notes from our phone conversation are in The File:

"You were set up"

"The way a case like this is defended [is to] dump on you"

"Leave [the firm] with your reputation intact"

"Don't risk [your next firm] finding out."

"No professional or financial upside [to filing suit]"

Palefsky asked me outright if I ever wanted to work in law again. I had just passed the grueling bar exam. My parents had just spent untold sums on three years of law school. I hadn't learned anything of substance in an entire year at Schiffer Mulligan. I couldn't yet truly evaluate whether I liked or had an aptitude for the job.

Yes, I wanted to work again.

I'd spent the last three years preparing for *this* job. If I wasn't a lawyer, what would I even do? How would I support myself? My terror grew.

I next met with Mark Rudy. In a letter after our face-to-face meeting, Rudy wrote that my claim was "meritorious" and his firm was willing to represent me in settlement negotiations with Schiffer Mulligan. "It seems to me that no one at Schiffer, Mulligan, et al., would want to air the issues involving your employment in a public forum," and he suggested mediation.

A few days later, as I was still debating what to do, I spoke to Rudy's associate on the phone to bounce settlement options off her. She responded with an impatient sigh, echoing what Palefsky had told me, "What, exactly, do you want?"

I want the firm to acknowledge that Mike's and Ben's and Tim's and Powell's and Brook's behavior was intolerable.

I want someone to say, "I'm sorry."

I want a decent, unmarred chance at being a lawyer.

I want someone to have my back, to say, "You're actually doing okay given the circumstances."

In Monica Lewinsky's "Emerging from 'The House of Gaslight' in the Age of #metoo" *Vanity Fair* article, she wrote, "I had been alone. *So. Very. Alone.* Publicly Alone — abandoned most of all by the key figure in the crisis, who actually knew me well and intimately. That I had made mistakes, on that we can all agree. But swimming in that sea of Aloneness was terrifying."

Swimming in a sea of Aloneness was precisely how I felt that entire year at Schiffer Mulligan.

The File contains Mark Rudy's billing statement from August 1994. I paid him $375 and abandoned any plans to take legal action against Schiffer Mulligan.

I was at a serious crossroads.

If I quit, how would I support myself?

How could I find a new job when, in 1994, it was virtually unheard of to switch firms after barely a year in practice?

How could I even explain to potential employers why I was job hunting? Wouldn't that trigger behind-the-scenes questions from potential firms to Schiffer Mulligan attorneys in San Francisco's incestuously intertwined legal community? Would Jasper Brook's uninformed characterization of my "interpersonal skills" follow me forever?

Even if a firm did consider hiring me after just one year of practice, how could I explain how little practical experience I'd gained in that year without, again, triggering a deeper dive into my time at Schiffer Mulligan?

Beyond potential employers, how would I explain to friends why I was making such an unorthodox, early shift?

How could I even search for a job while I was still under the gun to bill 1,900 hours at Schiffer Mulligan, the firm that insisted its workplace was *totally fine*?

How could I even come close to meeting that impossible standard when no one would give me work?

It had proven unsafe to come forward — at the firm and in the legal community more broadly — about what I was experiencing.

I'd never felt so misunderstood, lonely and trapped.

Chapter Eleven

2023

A doctor friend once told me about the phrase "true, true, but unrelated," a medical school concept indicating that two true facts aren't proof that they are related. We tend to assume, often wrongly, that events are causally connected simply if they happen together.

There's a related concept in law, known as the "even if" argument. For example, even if Chanel Miller made a poor choice to get blackout drunk on the Stanford campus, that did not give Brock Turner license to sexually assault her.

Many "even if" truths emerged as I re-examined my year at Schiffer Mulligan. I worked so hard to tell an accurate story, and I obsessed about tone. I risked relativizing pain by, for example, noting that Kelli's triumph over childhood sexual abuse triggered a re-examination of workplace trauma. I parsed every word as I threaded the needle between steering clear of sounding "victim-y" and undermining my awful experience. For my sort-seeking brain, the "even if" framework helped.

Even if, at 24, I was naive for falling for what someone once referred to as Mike's "act," *even if* I was immature, annoying, privileged, or entitled, I should not have been subjected to what I experienced as a hostile work environment.

Even if quid pro quo sexual harassment — the "having sex with me is your only chance at a promotion" — is worse, what I experienced over many months was in my mind still actionable gender-based harassment.

Even if some members of The Club sensed that Mike was full of shit when he disparaged me, *I* didn't know they knew that.

Even if you're going through a divorce or are abusing substances (like some Schiffer Mulligan attorneys were back then), you cannot discuss a female colleague's sex life or exclude her from firm events or deface her photo in your mutual place of employment.

Even if a different, more world-weary woman would have said, "Fuck him" and easily moved on from Mike, the broken-hearted way I reacted was equally understandable.

Even if there was no direct causal connection between Mike's badmouthing and The Club's conversations about me and my lack of work, the firm's mismanagement over my billable time prevented critical professional growth and my development as a lawyer.

Even if my experience in Big Law generally or at Schiffer Mulligan specifically wasn't the norm, the trauma of my experience is real.

Even if the intent of the inappropriate conversations among The Club was not malevolent, the effect still damaged my mental health and career. Just because someone doesn't mean harm does not mean harm isn't done.

Even if I wasn't an intuitive lawyer and *even if* Jasper Brook had legitimate reasons not to want me in the labor group, my personal life should never have been part of that assessment.

Even if good things happened in my life after I left Schiffer Mulligan— like meeting my husband through a connection at my next job — that year still caused tremendous pain, the effects of which I still feel.

Even if my story is not unique — after all, I'm certain women experience this behavior working at fast-food restaurants, hospitals, government agencies and non-profits — it's still important to tell.

Even if I would have failed in or left the law anyway, the career I'd spent three years preparing for was not theirs to take away.

In other words, the events of that year were indefensible.

***

In reporting my story, in building my "case," I spoke to experts in hostile work environments, power, gender, and women in law. I also interviewed more than a dozen former colleagues from Schiffer Mulligan. I reached out to individuals I expected would remember me and might have recollections about my interactions with The Club or my work product or both. In most cases I reached out by email, though for some hard-to-find or hard-to-reach sources I turned to Facebook or snail mail. I explained that I was working on a project about my first year as a lawyer, the years 1993-1994 at Schiffer Mulligan. I asked if they'd be willing to be interviewed, to discuss what they remembered from that time. Almost every former colleague I messaged agreed to be interviewed. And while I asked for availability for a "brief chat" (which I insisted take place over video so they could see my face, ensuring they'd accurately recollect who I was), almost every interview lasted at least an hour. The interviews appear here in the order in which I conducted them.

I had trouble sleeping in anticipation of many of the conversations. For some, I had to do meditations focused on cultivating courage beforehand. Seeing and talking with individuals from that time brought awful memories to the surface.

I deliberately chose not to record the video calls because I wanted interviewees to feel free to speak openly, and I suspected that recording them would inhibit their responses.

What I learned was infuriating — and validating.

VANESSA
Junior Associate

Vanessa was my very first interview for this project. She video called from a couch in what looked like a well-appointed home. My contemporary at the firm, Vanessa always seemed much older to me. She'd started at Schiffer Mulligan a bit before me but always seemed many miles ahead. Within minutes of first meeting her when I was a summer associate in 1992, for example, she made a joke about accidentally walking into Jasper Brook's office instead of her own. I had no idea who she was even talking about. I already felt behind.

A pretty and statuesque Latina woman with a thick Southern accent, Vanessa was engaged during my summer at Schiffer Mulligan and married by the time I started as a first-year associate in 1993. Vanessa and I didn't exactly bond, though I primarily attributed that to her being married and to her being in a completely different stage of life. Once, though, she came into my office freaking out because after doing a quick "search and replace" on a Word document, she'd somehow submitted a memo to a partner where almost every other word was "wart." We laughed about it together for weeks.

Vanessa and I were once pulled into a case to write several pre-trial motions requesting that certain evidence be kept from the jury. Before walking into the conference room to get instructions from the partner, I'd grabbed some candy from the receptionist's large jar and then proceeded, with my mouth full of Starbursts, to ask the partner whether so many motions would irritate the judge. As we walked out of the conference room, Vanessa whispered, "I wouldn't ask so many questions. Just do the work." At first, I was offended. *Who the hell does she think she is to tell me what to do?* But then I looked at the Starburst wrappers crumpled in my hand and felt about eight years old, my cheeks reddening with embarrassment. She was right.

During our 2023 Zoom call, Vanessa was thoughtful and refreshingly forthright. As uncomfortable as it was to hear her candid impressions of me back then, it was also healing because it proved that I had not imagined or inflated my deliberate exclusion from The Club. As a woman of color, she'd long been used to exclusion, she said, and knew it would be futile to try to join The Club. Instead, she just observed it.

How would you describe that time for young women in law?

[Long pause.]

There was a lot of promise, but still a sense of very real barriers to advancement. Not barriers to getting a job. Women could get jobs. But there was no thought of, "One day I'd like to become a partner." It wasn't realistic, being a person of color and female. I perceived the promise. But I lacked a sense of the monetary input required, of the importance of having clients, the economics. Also, I knew I was just not going to be "in the room where it happened."

If a young female was even remotely cute or attractive, that was the thing people commented on, about myself and others. It was not about our readiness to interface with clients. With men, they commented on whether he was a fun guy, and they parlayed that into fun with clients.

Describe the Schiffer Mulligan culture back then.

It was what most firms were: white, male dominated. The firm activities taking place were geared towards how fun was perceived from that viewpoint.

I wasn't upset about that. I'd witnessed things much worse. I spent the previous summer at another large firm, which was brutally, aggressively masculine. Schiffer was like a family, but a patriarchal family.

What were your memories of me back then?

What's top of mind — not to be offensive — is that it seemed like you were trying to fit into the boys club there, the Ben Bucknell group. That, to me, was what distinguished us. I didn't try. That didn't pan out perfectly for you and I wasn't surprised.

It seemed that you had dated Mike and he was very much in the group with the boys. He made it seem like you were trying to date him, kept sending out vibes and he was making it seem like you were making him settle down and have babies. I thought he was arrogant to presume that. He was turning it into something else — he treated you like a tagalong, like a little sister pest. I felt bad — this was your job, your career, and it was being affected by other peoples' comments, jokes, perceptions. I thought, "Why are they even a part of this?"

At that time, my expectations were much lower. Of course, you have to listen to dumb jokes. Now, I might get a little more angry about it. I wish someone who was older could have seen this and said, "This should not be taking place." It was overt, not unnoticeable.

There was mansplaining and toxic masculinity. These are not just terms by liberal media. They're real things and they keep other people from rising to their full potential. An older lawyer should have shut it down. It's unfortunate when older people who know better, who can guide a thing, don't. It makes me angry and disappointed.

TRACY

Best Friend

I further tiptoed into the memories of others from 1993 by texting Tracy, my best friend since high school, the friend who has seen me through everything — first loves, bad boyfriends, marriage, kids, everything — since I was 14. She's had a court-side seat for all of my life's biggest moments (and I to hers), from losing our virginity to the deaths of loved ones. In other words, Tracy has *context*. She also has an excellent memory. As I began to dig up the past, Tracy was one of my earliest sources. I trusted that she'd tell me if I'd been, as I long feared, ridiculous, pathetic and immature back then.

Erin:

Quick question for you: do you have any specific memories about my first year as a lawyer, the whole mess with the evil Mike, etc.? This was 1993-1994. It's related to my latest writing project. If you have no specific memories, I get it -- it was 30 years ago! However, if you do, I'd love to know what you remember me telling you about that time.

Tracy:

Lawyer memory... you writing xmas cards at work; women lawyers being mean to you; socializing didn't include you

Regarding evil Mike... at the time I was sad for you that you didn't make it to a '1 yr anniversary'. Now I look back and see how he took advantage of a young woman

Erin:

This is very helpful. How do you believe he took advantage, if you can recall?

Tracy:

I didn't feel that at the time. As I look back and I think about young women in the work force, I see how older men can take advantage of them

And I feel that happened with you

Erin:

Just out of curiosity, what did you feel at the time? That I was too sensitive? Or something else? (Be honest!)

Tracy:

At the time I WANTED you to find your person so badly. It was upsetting that it was just not happening

Absolutely did NOT feel you were being sensitive

With Tracy's affirmation, I continued to move forward, deepening my investigation into that time.

PATRICK

Mid-Level Associate

When we spoke by video call for this interview, Patrick had just turned 60 but still retained his preternaturally boyish appearance — with still-blond hair and a pre-teen's smile. He'd just retired from his longtime in-house counsel job.

A good friend of Mike, Patrick was the person with whom Mike had consulted about where to strategically place his overnight bag the first time he visited me in Los Angeles. Despite being squarely in The Club, Patrick always struck me as a decent enough guy. He ended up marrying a staff person he met at Schiffer Mulligan, a woman about my age named Sandy who I'd become friends with when I was a summer associate (again flouting the unspoken, invisible attorney-staff division). However, in our romantic breakup, Mike got both friends — Patrick and Sandy.

Patrick had been especially close to Mike back then and I had no idea whether they were still in contact. For all I knew, they've vacationed together every year. Therefore, even though Patrick had been friendly in our email exchanges beforehand, I was nervous about our interview.

What are your memories of me and Mike from that time?

I remember when you were dating Mike the four of us — you and Mike and me and Sandy — went out to dinner. It was a fun, youngish experience, a positive memory, a really fun evening for the four of us.

Mike and I were friends outside of work. We went mountain biking together. I remember we commiserated a lot back then about not liking the firm. About seven or eight years ago there was a Schiffer reunion. Mike was there. He's a big personality. Super engaging, fun, smart, funny.

What else do you remember about our relationship?

You were very enamored with him. I remember him being very into it and then seemingly kind of quickly he was aloof and distant, not sure how he felt. He characterized it as you being clingy. He felt suffocated.

Not to malign Mike, but I imagine he was a lot to handle. My memory is that it was an emotionally charged time.

He was filled with a lot of emotion. He would run hot and cold. He would be very into somebody and then not.

Not to psychoanalyze, but Mike was always struggling, with his family, his ambitions. He's divorced now. His wife was lovely, super smart. But it was a high emotion relationship.

Can you comment on the culture of the firm back then?

The "cast of characters" was a lot. Socializing in that era was different. We were young. The country was coming out of the Clarence Thomas hearings. There was awareness of overt sex harassment, but still not good recognition of the cultural stuff.

There was a big "bro" culture in that office. Bucknell really encouraged that bro-y thing. There was enablement. Things weren't called out. The stuff we would say...ugh. Part of it was the age we were and hopefully we've matured. A lot of stupid conversations happened and we didn't think about how different interactions affected people.

Like many sources, Patrick generously reminisced with me for almost an hour. But I was disappointed when he reminded me that during much of my first year at Schiffer Mulligan, he'd been sent by the firm to work on-site for one of Schiffer Mulligan's biggest clients down in Silicon Valley. So, while this interview was enlightening, he didn't quite have the bird's-eye view that I thought he would.

IRV

Junior Associate

Irv, along with Reggie, who I interviewed later, was one of the few bright spots during that awful year. Irv and Reggie were mid-level associates who, not long before I started at the firm, lateraled over to Schiffer Mulligan from Thelen Marrin Johnson & Bridges along with the rest of Thelen's environmental law group. They were funny and kind and smart and not even remotely interested in The Club. Irv, Reggie and I went to lunch together frequently, grabbed coffees at the candy shop downstairs. On weekends, we went to movies and author readings at bookstores. When Irv left Schiffer Mulligan in the spring — to do what he really wanted to do, which was to be on what he calls "the good side" of environmental litigation — I sensed that there probably could be no happy future for me there.

Irv moved to New York City a few years after leaving Schiffer Mulligan and today has his own law practice. He video conferenced from his office and it was one of the few interviews that I wasn't nervous about. Connecting with a friend who had stood by me at a painful time filled me with joy.

What do you remember about Schiffer Mulligan then?

Not much because I really didn't integrate into the culture there. I never wanted to work at a big firm. I didn't even want to move there from Thelen. I just wanted to do environmental law.

What do you remember about my situation with Mike?

He was part of that male, bro culture that wasn't different from any other law firm or any male-dominated office in 1993. To me, it was no worse than Thelen.

I didn't hear anything around the office about you two. It was all from you. I heard you'd been dating Mike, you were going to live together, you broke up. He was in the good graces of the firm, in with the partners. He was the popular kid in the firm. I vaguely remember you having a hard time because of Mike.

Any other memories from that time?

We all kind of hated it there in our own way. The big firm culture was bad in a lot of ways. And for sensible, nice, considerate, caring people like us, none of us liked those big firms and the big corporate clients. There were all sorts of bad things there.

LYNN

Sexual Harassment Attorney and Family Friend

After I was surreptitiously handed the Brook memo, from which I inferred I was being set up to fail, my parents suggested that I speak with their longtime friend Lynn. She'd spent her career as an employment lawyer for several federal agencies, handling employment discrimination complaints. In fact, a big part of her work was claims of hostile work environment, especially sexual harassment. It was Lynn who guided me about what to say when I confronted managing partner Frederick Duncan days after being handed the Brook memo.

Do you remember me calling you during that time?

Yes. I remember you'd had a relationship with a guy, a star there at the firm, and then him breaking it off. After that, you were dissatisfied in how you were treated, the assignments you got. People stopped talking to you. You had dual emotional upheavals.

[I recounted several of the events of that year.] Does this, in your opinion, meet the standards of a hostile work environment?

For sure it was a hostile work environment.

The standard is: how would reasonable women in that position react in the same or similar circumstances?

What you experienced sounds outrageous and purposefully cruel. The work environment, the taking sides, not being invited to things, the attitudes are heavily loaded on the side of men.

It's what a lot of women were up against. It certainly derailed the path you were primed to take. You never got the support or the development you needed.

A hostile work environment is treating one group of people differently. They were doing this to drive you out. They gave you no help. They created this intolerable environment that you couldn't exist in.

And the fact that you were later told "if you raise this [in court], you'll never have a job again" was correct and was what women were up against. Most whistleblowers' professional lives are undone and they're unspokenly banned from whatever profession they're in.

When I spoke to Lynn in 2023 to get her recollections of our conversations from 1994, she suggested I read Frances Conley's book, which turned out to be a model for me in writing about my experience in law. Conley's brave, personal account of the hostile work atmosphere, *Walking Out on the Boys* used a combination of real names and highly transparent pseudonyms and landed on the Bay Area's best seller list. Her candid recollections, which shredded her colleagues and superiors, starkly showed that, despite some gains, women in medicine were still considered inferior and, as a result, women's health care suffered. Once again, I can thank Lynn for excellent advice — in dealing with a hostile work environment and in gathering inspiration for my own writing project.

REGGIE

Mid-Level Associate

I'm so proud of Reggie — of "Reggie and Irv" — who, after a long career at the US Attorney's Office, is now a judge. Like Irv, Reggie had come over to Schiffer Mulligan as part of the environmental law group from Thelen, Marrin, Johnson & Bridges. He is Japanese-American, one of the few attorneys of color at the firm at that time.

It was Reggie who happened to come into my office mere moments after the secretary slipped me the Jasper Brook memo. It was Reggie who observed me trembling, who explained to me what "Marvin'd" meant. His rage on my behalf, the seriousness in his eyes helped me understand that I was not overreacting to the Brook memo. It was Reggie who reported the full-body trembling I experienced upon reading the memo to Dixon Long, the Schiffer Mulligan partner who later insisted that I had not, in fact, experienced a hostile work environment.

As with Irv, talking with Reggie was a soul booster. He was hilarious, smart and insightful.

What do you remember about Schiffer Mulligan then?

I was very thankful to have you and Irv there as peers. We had the same kind of experience, not having enough work, getting one of those "you need to bill 300 hours — fill in the blank — a month until the end of the year." I get it. It's a business. I, at least, had support from the people I worked with, the people I came from Thelen with. They were very good to me.

We all needed hours. Then you see Mike walking around like, "I don't have any problem getting work."

What memories do you have of me from that time?

I vividly remember you suffering, in part because of personal circumstances and it was really hard on you. I cannot imagine how that would be. The first job out of law school is so critical, so formative. Big Law is not particularly nurturing especially if you don't fit the mold. You just try to survive and learn to be a lawyer. I thought you maintained yourself incredibly well outwardly.

Dealing with the work environment, the dynamic is difficult. Law firms have their pets. Mike was a straight, white man. He was the golden child and the firm was fawning over him. Ben Bucknell? You could see who he liked. It was a "bro factory" so they would always feel more comfortable with someone like Mike. It felt like a fraternity because of their collegiality. They liked to tease each other, party, do things on the weekends. But some of those jokes from others — they can terrorize associates!

It happened at Thelen too. Definitely the men felt more comfortable, were more quickly viewed as one of them when it came time to assigning cases. There's an affinity. That's certainly how partners are made: those little intangible interactions.

We were all trying to get hours and be productive and you were also worried about getting work because of your personal circumstances. I remember you were keeping a file because you were very much worried how you would be reviewed and treated. I remember thinking, "How smart." It seemed proactive, keeping emails. I have a vivid memory of your fucking stack of emails!

For a good chunk of time, you were definitely feeling a lot of anxiety about how you were being treated — in contrast to how Mike was being treated. You worked very hard to maintain yourself outwardly but you were suffering inwardly.

Thirty years later, I can't imagine how you were even functioning. As a junior associate in even the best of circumstances, there's a baseline level of insecurity — Are they being fair to me? Am I being a good lawyer? — because when you're beginning as a lawyer, we don't know shit. And that's not even going through what you went through. It was grim. I cannot imagine. And then to get the memo that corroborated your fear that they're talking about you. You were *just* getting started. I feel sorry for you. I imagine it was so hard on you and I commend you for facing this, bearing it, living with it, and making peace with it.

How do you look at that time now, with a 2023 lens?

On a Zoom screen now of the lawyers who appear before me, it's still all men. Law is unforgiving. It can be a grim existence. The plum jobs don't go to women or people of color. It's a strained and strange environment.

I remember at firms people would say, "You could always join [the elite crowd]." But what are you going to do? Invite a partner to lunch or drinks? They'd view you as a freak! And as women or non-white men, it's even more difficult. There are micro aggressions. But the culture is to bury it. Diversity, Equity and Inclusion committees at firms? I'm cynical. It's cosmetic.

SCOTT
Senior Associate

Scott is small, stocky and completely bald. He looks like — and is — the kind of guy who might grab someone by the throat and threaten them to stop being a jerk. But Scott is also the kind of guy who's secretly a huge teddy bear with a great sense of humor and a heart of gold. Scott was not a litigator, and though he is a "guy's guy," he wasn't part of The Club — he was more Club Adjacent.

I'd forgotten that, like boyish-looking Patrick who'd been sent on-site to a client, Scott spent some of 1993-1994 out of the office. He was seconded — sent to work temporarily in another fast-paced legal environment to gain trial skills. Still, Scott had important insight.

He video conferenced from his office and we talked for a long, long time.

What do you remember about me?

I remember you faintly as eager, bright. There was nothing negative. I never had a problem with you. I remember you had dated Mike and there was an ugly breakup and the guys took his side. I was not one hundred percent shocked.

I had very limited interactions with Mike. I came across guys like him before. He was in his orbit with Bucknell and Tim Reids. I didn't think he was a bad guy. We just didn't connect.

I have a sense that I only know the tip of the iceberg of what happened to you. It's hard to hear. You're onto something [with this book], but it's gotta be nuanced.

What do you remember about Bucknell, Tim Reids and that cast of characters?

So much of a law firm experience depends on the partners you're assigned to. It's all about where you happen to get slotted in that office. I was in a totally different world. I knew them casually. They had their own thing going and occasionally I'd see part of it.

Without diminishing your experience, I reject the premise of the firm being a unified front. We were different islands. That said, if you land on the wrong one, you've got a problem. It's like surfing: there's a one in ten thousand chance that a shark will get you, but if you're the one, those odds don't matter.

At Schiffer Mulligan, the shark got you.

Honestly, most of the lawyers there were fighting their own set of wars. There were divorces, partners having problems with management because their behavior caused them to go through associates. Nearly everyone who worked at Schiffer left for different circumstances so don't think that it's all milk and honey. You'd be a lot less dazzled by them if you knew that most were hanging by a thread. Many of those partners paid, but not necessarily for that crime [they committed against you].

I look back on that time and don't think of it as a monochrome time. A lot of women flourished there, including two who were my supervisors. Why? Because the shark didn't get them.

KIMBERLY

Mid-Level Associate

Ever since Mike told me that Kimberly criticized my first-day suit choice, I was never sure if she was friend or foe. While not in The Club, she was the kind of woman The Club liked — irreverent, foul-mouthed, a woman who could hold her own. Even when I interviewed Kimberly for this book, she referred to Mike as "'Baum," his nickname at Schiffer Mulligan. Because of this, I was nervous to talk with her, despite her friendly email in reply to my request for an interview.

But during our conversation, I learned a lot. I even asked her point-blank about the suit comment. She didn't remember but, importantly, she also didn't deny it. "That sounds like something I might say," she admitted, which I admired and made me trust her.

Spiky-haired and no-nonsense, Kimberly had a self-awareness and self-confidence in her abilities that I wondered if I, too, would have gained if it weren't for the experiences I had at the firm.

In many ways, Kimberly is like me. She's got a what-you-see-is-what-you-get personality, but hers comes with a tough-as-nails edge. At 58, Kimberly still handles complex litigation as a solo practitioner, noting, unabashedly, that she's good at it. She describes law firm life as "hard core — you sink or swim and I was a swimmer." When she was a first-year (at the firm she was at before Schiffer Mulligan), she was even allowed to argue a $5 million bankruptcy case, a far cry from the paltry work I was given.

What do you remember about Schiffer Mulligan at that time?

I was only there two years. I came over with a group from Baptiste Beaumont. Schiffer was more of a blue-chip firm, but it was an easy job.

A lot of us younger folks got along really well. I worked with people I came over with. A Schiffer associate on our staff commented that we worked really hard and were demanding. There was nothing bad about the Schiffer quality of work — it was just more country club-ish and cozy.

It was totally a bro culture. And Ben — I think the world of Ben. As individuals, they were just fine but not when they came together. They were good-looking, white, twenty-something-year-olds, some providers for a family, on their way to what they saw as their road to partnership. There was a group factor.

What do you remember about me?

You were extremely eager, a pleaser, lovely. You were trying to find your way. You were getting inconsistent work, being pushed around from person to person. You were looking for a home.

Maybe we worked together on a project basis. You were extremely outgoing, a pleasure. You were trying to figure out who you were and you were not getting answers.

You were super eager. You went out of your way to try to ask, "Can I help you? Can I do these things?" I remember nothing negative.

You cannot say your work was shit when you're a baby lawyer. No one is allowed to be called shit until they've practiced for a few years. A lot of people didn't know what they were doing.

Do you remember anything about Mike and me?

He was one of the bros. I remember something happened [between you]. Nothing you're saying surprises me because he was fooling around with everyone. [Makes disparaging comment about his appearance.] In retrospect, what were you thinking?

I do not remember you as a basket case or as a crazy ex-girlfriend.

There was a ton of shit going on, inappropriate conduct and relationships. It was not just you. It was widespread.

What do you think about it now, in 2023?

I didn't think about gender until I got older. I had not one female mentor. I wasn't sensitive or petrified — you either had what it took or didn't, but for me it wasn't along gender lines.

All of those lawyers were a similar type. There was a bro-hood but not entirely based on gender. There was no tolerating and accepting diversity of personality, viewpoints, world outlooks. You have to be okay looking. You're trained, "This is the way you do it." There was nothing outside the box. The men I know who have succeeded are all the same, all white men.

I was outspoken and I'd curse at Baptiste Beaumont. I'd be told, "That doesn't fit our protocol. You can't bring in clients by talking like that." But that's exactly why clients liked me.

If you'd continued at the firm, you would have hated it. It's a miserable business. All I do is move money around. I hate it but I realize I dug my hole. I do love solving problems and seeing an issue that no one else sees. But it's too late to do something else. I make much less money now on my own, but I don't want to deal with the administration of Big Law. The competition there is the worst. It's ego driven. Everyone wants to be considered important by clients and by the firm.

We all identify so much with our careers. When your career is undermined, it undermines everything about yourself. I'm horrified, sick to my stomach about what happened to you. It's sad and eye-opening. Good for you for taking power over this.

MAX

Mid-Level Associate

I can't listen to George Michael's "Freedom" without thinking of Max and the summer of 1992, when I was a summer associate at Schiffer Mulligan, and Max was a junior associate with a new Mercedes Benz convertible. On one particularly bluebird day, Max and some other associates took me, Brian, (another associate in my class, a wonderful man who was and remains a kind and supportive friend), and others over to Sam's, the legendary outdoor burger place right on the water in Sausalito. "Lunch" lasted about three hours and "Freedom" blared from Max's stereo system as we drove back over the Golden Gate Bridge with the top down, our bellies full of burgers and fries and our cheeks pink from sunshine.

Max was — and still is — a pretty boy akin to Rob Lowe. Today, Max lives in New England. After leaving the law, he got an MBA and transitioned to international consulting. He has four kids, including a daughter who's the age I was when I started at Schiffer Mulligan.

I was surprised Max agreed to talk with me because he was absolutely, 100 percent within The Club. And I'm grateful for his honest recollections about The Club.

Describe Schiffer Mulligan during that time.

I was completely consumed in document review and low-level depositions all over the Pacific Northwest. I was in Seattle almost every week. I thought, "This is awful. I don't want to do this. I don't want to be these partners. This is not interesting. It's tedious." I was not in a healthy place. I remember getting hammered every Friday. Mentally, I was already looking to do something else.

Do you remember anything about the Ben Bucknell crowd?

Of course, I was *in* that crowd! There was a lot of fun and jocularity. My best memories were Fridays at Chevy's at Four Embarcadero. Patrick and I would get martinis. The group was great. I liked those people and we're still in touch.

Do you remember conversations that might, today, be considered inappropriate?

Oh my God, *of course* there were those conversations. That was thirty years ago, before the woke-fest arrived. There was a lot of off-color stuff. And of course it was about people who worked there. Looking back, I don't remember it being mean-spirited or seriously misogynistic or chauvinist or racist, but we did talk a lot of trash.

[David] Powell could be irreverent and was always starting conversations. I do remember Mike Davenbaum talking about your rent situation. But he said a lot of things about a lot of people.

My take on Mike is that he was well-liked because he was funny and fun. But it could be a little too much. He had to be the loudest guy in the room. I remember a couple of times thinking, "I'm gonna leave now." He was a bit of a drama queen, but we teased him about it. He got teased a lot. Partly it was junior hazing and partly he invited some of it because he could take it. It was classic frat stuff.

I don't remember your situation at Schiffer, but would I be surprised? No.

What do you remember about me?

You struck me as a pretty friendly person. You were cute, nice looking, an attractive person. I don't remember having lengthy conversations with you. I don't remember you being at a lot of after-hours events. You weren't a basket case or obsessed. But I was in my own world. At least Bucknell was involved so there was some humanity. He allowed me to argue a 10th Circuit appeal in Denver that we knew we were going to lose. That was the thing — we chased every appeal to make more money.

[I gave him my account of my year there.]

That's terrible, awful. It was mistreatment. I'd ask a lot of questions of a lot of people. They can't hide behind "that was then." I'm sorry that's how your year went. I wish I could remember more.

DENISE

Mid-Level Associate

Denise is someone whose path I've crossed many times since Schiffer Mulligan. I first got to know her back when I was a summer associate in 1992 and she was my associate mentor. (This was a titular role only — she didn't mentor me work-wise. Rather, she was there if I had questions about the summer associate internship program or about Big Law generally.)

She was a transactional lawyer so we didn't work together, but one of my strongest memories of her that summer is seeing her crying as she came down the outside escalator at the Embarcadero at the end of the day. When Denise spotted me observing her, she didn't try to hide her rage and explicitly attributed it to the male partner she worked closely with.

Years later, in the early 2000's, Denise and I began running into each other at Laurel Village, an old-fashioned mini mall in San Francisco — often called Fertility Village or Stroller Village. In fact, at that time, we were both new moms, each with a boy and a girl just a year apart. Years later, we ran into each other while touring kindergartens for our boys. Our kids are in college now, but I continue to run into her periodically at Laurel Village.

A tiny woman with a ready smile, Denise can best be described as sweet, spending her time these days volunteering with her church and in other organizations. She knew herself and her reputation as a genteel goody-goody and, like Vanessa, didn't even try to infiltrate The Club. When we spoke in 2023, she was thoughtful in her responses, often closing her eyes as she spoke.

What do you remember about Schiffer Mulligan during that time?

I was struggling with my own career choices. I knew life wasn't going the way I wanted but I couldn't take time to discern if it was me, this firm, or this practice because all I was doing was working.

As for the culture there, my perspective now is that it was very much a young white man's world. When I was interviewing, I was shocked I got an offer because the two young associates who interviewed me were clearly smart but total jocks and I left the interview thinking, "This is not my world." I was not put off — I had been a paralegal at another firm, which was even more of an old boys' network — but I was aware of it.

I was happy to see women like Elizabeth, who seemed strong and they were making it there. But women with power didn't look out for women with no power. If anyone was LGBTQ, they would have been miserable in that environment. You had to be a man's man.

I remember some of those guys would get on the PA system late at night and sing the phrase "Bad to the Bone" because of some inside joke. I just wanted to do my work. People didn't ostracize me but I wasn't part of the in-crowd.

Ben was the head of recruiting and was always cheerleading for social stuff. He got passed up for partner at first. Back then standard was seven years [to make partner] but it was shifting to longer and he got hit with that shift. He made it the second time. It didn't help that San Francisco was considered the stepsister office after L.A., San Diego and Orange County.

What do you remember about me?

As a summer associate, you were hard-working, eager to learn and involved. You came to events, you didn't shy away. I thought you would be a good hire. I don't remember your actual work product because I was a transactional lawyer. But I was involved in recruitment and everybody thought you did good work or you wouldn't have gotten an offer.

Do you remember anything about the situation with me and Mike?

Mike was very gregarious. He was like a big puppy — he was gangly, he didn't know his space, his boundaries. He needed to grow up. His prefrontal cortex was not developed. He was definitely part of that go-out-for-drinks associates crowd.

As for conversations about you two, people didn't talk about some things when I was around. People thought of me like a mom. In some ways, it was a sign of respect, but it also meant that I was not included in certain things. Sometimes it's easier to be on the outside.

[I recounted my Schiffer Mulligan story.]

You were made to be inconsequential, not a human. We used to say we were all "fungible billing units," but this was even worse. You were just an object. The culture there remains: some people are disposable.

In my church, we were searching for a new bishop and we learned from sociologists to examine what someone prizes on the spectrum of community-to-individuality. At the firm, there was no sense of community if you were outside the in-crowd.

Addressing this is brave and wise. If you can reclaim your sense of self by writing? That's a win.

Your story sheds light on a particular snapshot in time and it hasn't changed. If you're a rich white guy with enough connections? You can still do whatever you want. Power is seductive and there will be white male leadership in power structures forever. They still don't get it and we're all disadvantaged by it.

I'm so sorry this happened to you and countless others. It never should have happened. It's a systemic issue.

ELIZABETH

Partner, Also in Charge of San Francisco Associate Reviews

This interview was one of the most nerve-wracking and, it turns out, one of the most critical to my understanding of the firm.

Elizabeth was one of the few female partners at Schiffer Mulligan's San Francisco office in 1993, a woman of power, a woman others talked about. And they're talking about her still.

Kimberly (of the suit comment) referenced Elizabeth as being involved in one of the firm's "biggest scandals." According to Kimberly during our 2023 interview, Elizabeth was considered a "favorite son" by the powers that be, known for being hardworking, diligent, and an effective litigator — for a time. And then rumors swirled that she allegedly "ran away from the firm" after allegedly billing "fake hours."

During my video call with Max, The Club's pretty boy, he called Elizabeth "crazy," a lawyer who "never seemed to be in the office except from one to four a.m." He recalled that there was "a lot of talk about her being in a relationship with someone to keep her there because no one thought she was any good. She was very difficult to work with. Everything was very last minute. She was just a politician." Max even went so far as to call her "mentally imbalanced."

My friend Reggie, the now-judge, recalled that when he gave notice at Schiffer Mulligan to go work at a prestigious government office, Elizabeth came into his office and said, "I always wanted to go [work where you're going] but I can't leave because I can do whatever I want here because I'm a partner."

Others called Elizabeth "a piece of work" and "very unreliable."

To me, she'd seemed very much part of the in-crowd. She hosted firm parties at her house. Everyone knew and talked about Elizabeth. She spent a lot of time in the firm's main office in Los Angeles where the biggest power players were.

When I was a first-year, I was terrified of Elizabeth. I was also angry with her and the few other women partners for tacitly permitting The Club's antics. Their conversations were not a secret. After all, if *I*, someone so on the outside of everything knew about them, then everyone did.

I resented Elizabeth and the other women partners for failing to at the very least check in with me and the other young women to see how life was panning out for us at their firm. A tiny bit of kindness or interest would have gone a long way for me and other women. This kind of outreach might have even changed the trajectory of what happened later at Schiffer Mulligan.

Elizabeth had the important job of being the partner in charge of associate reviews. As such, I felt that she was squarely responsible for me not getting my six-month review until after the 10-month mark, even though I'd requested a review starting on the precise day of my six-month anniversary. I'd always assumed Elizabeth's delay was deliberate, a way to keep me down. When I finally did receive my written reviews, she wouldn't let me take the papers out of her office. Instead, I had to frantically scribble notes while sitting at her side table. She hurried me along, telling me that she had to leave momentarily. I was too afraid to object and, not surprisingly, I wasn't able to write everything down before it was time for her to leave. I was too intimidated to ask to see them again later.

I was shocked when Elizabeth agreed to be interviewed for this book. When we logged onto Zoom, I thanked her for agreeing to speak with me. She replied, "I'm the number one evangelist for getting out of law. I'm very bullish about that. Good for you, Erin! You got over the wall!"

Elizabeth's friendly, upbeat, congratulatory tone confounded me. Then it hit me: *she doesn't remember me.*

Describe Schiffer Mulligan at that time.

I worked a lot out of the L.A. office and I was not a fan of the L.A. culture. There was a lot of misogyny. Yet I wanted to fit in — I'd giggle at jokes that minimized my gender. I wonder now, did I have Stockholm Syndrome? It should never have been like that.

I realized I didn't like my partners. They drank too much, got divorced, spent more money than they made. Plus, litigators fought for a living, which is miserable.

I tried to fit in. There was a heavy drinking culture and drinking was a large part of my life there. It's one of the things I don't like about myself. A shrink told me back then that I had to go to a rehab clinic before he'd treat me. That scared me. When you get out of the pond of lawyers, you see that most people don't drink that much.

When I think back on my wish to fit in, to keep up with the men, I think, "What an idiot, Elizabeth." I was in an alcoholic fog the whole time. And I did have a bad exit at Schiffer. I believe in owning your role in problems.

I tried to speak out about abuses I saw there once I became a partner. I was naive and got pummeled. I was ostracized. Suddenly, I had no work. It happened so quickly. Frankly, I wasn't tough enough. I negotiated an exit. I thought, "I'm not going silently," but then they asked for a release.

I was scarred by that and I pushed it out of my mind. It was such an injurious journey for me, I shut down. It was too painful to think about because it knocked me on my ass.

I'd come in [to law practice] optimistic, eager to please, thinking, "I can't wait to prove myself." Then I was just decimated in a way I didn't understand. It was a river of despair that went through me for the longest time.

It was very dark. I didn't know what to do. I was deeply unhappy and didn't work for half a year. Then I ran out of money.

I went to work at a shitty hellhole, a manufacturing plant in a bad part of Oakland, a contrast to my corner office at Schiffer. I was downwardly mobile. I was an HR person there and paid a pittance but I loved it. Later, [through various iterations of the company], I became general counsel and VP of HR.

When I became a single mom, I took a job at a Japanese healthcare company closer to home and my career took off. I worked my way up to CEO and president of the holding company.

What do you remember about the culture of the San Francisco office, in particular?

It was a jock culture there, no doubt about that. Ben was a nice guy and part of that cabal there. He fit in the dominant culture. He was not the brightest. I always felt I could run circles around him. I remember the big red bow on the red sports car he got his wife. I never believed the appearances.

Do you remember Dixon Long from the Los Angeles office?

Oh gawwwwddd. [Look of disgust.] I heard from a friend that Schiffer paid a lot of money in a harassment settlement. [Note: Because most settlements are subject to non-disclosure agreements, Elizabeth's assertion is not one I could confirm.] I became obsessed with learning the details. I feel like I never avenged the wrongdoing. I was too afraid to talk about it. I wanted to know they were punished.

The #metoo movement changed my life. Never in my life did I think this [reckoning] would happen. We're a subjugated gender — I figured, that was my fate, that we should be lucky for the crumbs we get in life.

After speaking with Elizabeth, I was frozen. My mind swam. I had to lie down. I was utterly exhausted. And ashamed. I realized during our call that I'd been doing to Elizabeth what everyone had done to me. Even in 2023, I'd laughed when my sources called Elizabeth "crazy." I'd been sorting people the way I sorted laundry, the precise way Schiffer lawyers had slotted me into a "crazy ex-girlfriend" column.

Elizabeth is eccentric, to be sure. She talks fast and goes on long, wild tangents. But she was *not crazy*. In fact, she was brutally, admirably honest about her flaws and her internalized misogyny.

Despite her not remembering me, after I explained my own Schiffer Mulligan trajectory during the end of our Zoom interview, Elizabeth acknowledged that what happened at the firm "completely derailed [my] life plan." Then, a few hours later, she followed up with an email:

"Hello Erin

I am sorry I was not more 'friendly' to you back then. To be honest, I had no recollection of knowing you — other than your name was familiar. I assumed you were in the L.A. office.

And I also had no idea that the fellows in the SF office were so abusive. I guess I saw them as annoying and harmless jocks — but boy was I wrong.

And keep in mind, I was in my own hell, but that is no excuse.

I really want to support you in your book. And you have inspired me to unpack a bit myself."

I was so grateful Elizabeth agreed to speak with me. Processing our conversation, I realized — thanks to her raw honesty — that she'd simply been doing at Schiffer Mulligan what I'd been trying to do: fit into a hostile crowd. Even at her high level, Elizabeth had also been professionally and emotionally harmed by Schiffer Mulligan's patriarchal culture.

Her experience shows that so many women are subjected to hostile work environments and, back then at least, failed to help each other. And that created a chain reaction. In the sink or swim environment that is Big Law, if a high-level woman is sinking, then that drastically reduces the chances of women "below" her to swim.

This shattering interview reminded me that although I'm no longer in a hierarchical institution, I can still extend my hand to other women by sharing my story, exactly the way the stories of my friend Kelli, Monica Lewinsky, Stanford rape victim Chanel Miller, and Frances Conley, the doctor who resigned in protest from Stanford Medical School, helped me.

Other women might be inclined to minimize their experiences in hostile work environments. After all, we tell ourselves, it's not childhood abuse like what happened to Kelli or the kind of quid pro quo sexual harassment of being forced to perform sexual acts to avoid negative consequences on the job. But the constant attacks on self-esteem, being demeaned and gaslit by men in positions of power are still an awful, cut-by-cut professional death.

We must stop dismissing our own suffering.

We must stop trying to excuse or ignore bad behavior.

We must speak out and help each other.

FREDERICK

Managing Partner of the San Francisco Office

And now we come to Frederick Duncan.

The managing partner at Schiffer Mulligan when everything went down, Duncan's name came up during several interviews with other lawyers.

One person described him as "awful."

Another said that, when meeting Duncan, "my finely tuned asshole detector went off like a car alarm."

Another lawyer who worked directly with him said, "We were walking lines I wouldn't walk anymore. It was evil, the devil's work. He had a lot of work at Schiffer Mulligan, but if you look at the merits of that work — there was a lot of unnecessary litigation, litigation he perpetuated that didn't need to be perpetuated." In other words, this lawyer was alleging that Duncan pursued legal avenues he knew were fruitless simply to bill more hours. (Note: I found no formal disciplinary complaints against Duncan on the California State Bar website or elsewhere.)

Needless to say, I was as shocked that Duncan agreed to speak with me as I was when Elizabeth did. I slept fitfully for several nights before our scheduled interview.

Did he remember me crying in his office?

Had he, sometime in the last 30 years, reconsidered Dixon Long's callous rejection of my claim of a hostile work environment?

In my mind, even all these years later, he was still the managing partner, and I the lowliest associate.

Now in his 80's, Duncan works in the energy field. On the video call, he looked like a kindly grandfather in his red zip-up fleece and now white hair.

What do you remember about Schiffer Mulligan at that time?

I try not to think about Schiffer Mulligan. It was not a happy parting. The whole thing was quite an experience. The people I brought with me [from Baptiste Beaumont] also left.

Some sources have called it a "bro factory." Do you agree?

We used to call them cliques. It was one of the problems in the office: people didn't work together well.

Do you remember me talking with you about a hostile work environment?

There were lots of tensions in the labor group. I don't register specifics. It was stressful for everyone.

Do you remember receiving this memo from Jasper Brook? [I read him the memo.]

I don't recall anything. Can you email that to me so I can take a closer look? [I emailed the text of the memo while we were on the call.]

The litigation group was busy that year but if you didn't have work, I have a hunch that it was simply because you wouldn't have had the experience to pick up complex, advanced cases.

I clashed a lot with Brook and he and I exchanged a lot of thoughts. He was making life difficult for all of us. He had his finger in as much as he could to ingratiate himself with [certain clients].

I heard he was disbarred. [Note: I sought to confirm this claim, but Brook's official California Bar status is "Resigned," effective the same year he was suspended for failure to pay dues and failure to comply with mandatory continuing education requirements.]

[I told Frederick about everything I had done to get work that year.] Was there anything else a first-year associate could have done to increase my hours?

I can't think of anything.

Do you recall summoning Dixon Long from the Los Angeles office to come investigate my assertion that I'd been in a hostile work environment?

I don't recall.

Do you have any recollection of me?

I have no negative impression. I worked with a number of associates who really didn't cut it and we had to ask them to leave. But you weren't among them.

Schiffer was a mixture of talent — some were capable and some were not and some were not hardworking.

[It became increasingly clear that Frederick did not remember me at all. I went on to describe in detail what I experienced that year.]

Belatedly, I'm sorry. There's no good reason for it all. You were just too junior. That's too bad. I'm sorry that occurred.

When I logged off of the Zoom call, I told my husband about our conversation. Using names from his own career, I hypothesized how my husband would react if it was clear that lawyers who'd played a critical role in his career and emotional state didn't even remember him.

"I would feel," he said, in a sad tone, "insignificant."

Exactly.

I get that it was 30 years ago, and Frederick is now in his 80's and it didn't happen to him. But was a young woman so unhappy with his supervision that she was *crying* in his office so commonplace as to be unmemorable?

The day after I spoke to Frederick in 2023, I emailed him a PDF of a letter I had in The File. It was dated 1994, sent upon my departure from Schiffer Mulligan. I was compelled to write the letter after, on my last day, Frederick reiterated that I had not experienced a hostile work environment at Schiffer Mulligan. I'd cc'd Jasper Brook, Dixon Long and the managing partner of the entire firm. In emailing the PDF, I asked Frederick to read it and give me his 2023 thoughts.

That 1994 letter read, in part:

"Dear Frederick:

You mentioned on the day that I gave notice that the firm and I see things differently. This comment disturbed me and I would like to let you know how I see my year at Schiffer, Mulligan.

As Ben Bucknell once put it to me, I started at the firm '0 for 2.'... I began work in October with associates warning me about [inappropriate conversations about a personal relationship that] had taken place [among partners and associates the summer before I started working].

As you know, the department to which I was assigned was extremely slow when I started. I did not receive a partner 'mentor' responsible for my hours until several months later. As I showed you and Dixon Long, I kept a record of every time I asked for work. Despite my low hours and consistent requests for work, there was no initiative to move me into a busier department or otherwise see to it that my hours were met. I'm not sure what more a first-year associate was to do....

I complained to a partner about the inappropriate conversations taking place. Though I was characteristically assured that things would improve, they did not. As I told you before, Mike threatened to 'ruin my career' at Schiffer (it can be argued that he was successful) and threatened to use his position on the recruiting committee to not give my summer associate mentee an offer because of our troubled relationship. When I told a partner that Mike had threatened me, the partner stated, 'I don't doubt it.'

Meanwhile, I had a series of articles published in legal newspapers which I always intended to be something positive for the firm. Indeed, I have attached just some of the letters I received in response to one of the articles. I only very recently found out that some partners were not happy with the articles. While this attitude surprised me, I was even more surprised that no one told me they felt this way. I would have been more than happy to not publish later articles, or at least not mention Schiffer, Mulligan's name. One day I walked by one of the articles which my secretary had posted in the copy center and noticed that it had been defaced.

Beginning in April, I asked for my 6-month review. I was persistent with this request (ask Sally Bucklin) because I was disturbed by my low hours and my still working on a project-by-project basis. [Footnote: Jasper's E-mail mentioned that you and he had to cut some of my hours. This is largely the result of the fact that, due to the poor management over my time, I was almost always pulled into cases completely unfamiliar to me at the very last minute.] I knew my review was the forum to air these concerns. I did not receive my

6-month review until August. [Footnote: As you know, this review was quite favorable. In addition, I have heard you were impressed with the memo I wrote for you.]

In late spring, Tim Reids was planning the Tahoe trip. Tim would not accept my simple 'no' for an answer and insisted on knowing why I wasn't going. Rather than lie, I told him that I didn't want to be around Mike for an entire weekend (i.e., I did not suggest that I was busy that weekend). Subsequently, Mike gave notice to the firm. Unfortunately, the feeling was not "Great, now Erin, who still works here and who is actually a mentor for a summer associate can come." Rather, it was arranged for Mike to attend the Tahoe trip [anyway], paid by the firm, despite the fact that he had not worked at the firm for two weeks. Similarly, although I had told Ben Bucknell that I was afraid of Mike, he was invited to the end-of-summer party after he left the firm.

Despite all of this, when Mike left, I was willing to let a lot of these incidents slide. Then Jasper Brook's E-mail was brought to my attention. While initially I thought the firm was taking the matter seriously by conducting an investigation, I was appalled at the nastiness and partiality of the 'investigation.' I (and others) found Dixon Long's tone to be accusatory and skeptical and not at all neutral. This is when I decided to seek independent legal advice.

The result of the firm's investigation was negligible. The most I ever got was that the firm was sorry that I had seen the E-mail, not sorry that it had been written. From what I can tell, despite the fact that this incident was just as serious as Ron's 'shoe throwing' incident, Jasper did not even receive a slap on the wrist for sexist and entirely inappropriate behavior. In the meantime, my few friends left at the firm were given subtle signals to disassociate themselves from me for 'political' reasons. Unfortunately, some of them did.

My workload subsequently increased and I feel that I finally got a chance to show my stuff with the [client name] case. Don has told me he agrees. I really thought that Schiffer, Mulligan was a place I could work successfully for several years and I hoped to do great things there. I may not be the greatest legal mind to grace San Francisco. However, I think I had a successful combination of qualities. For instance, I know that [client name], [client name], and [client name] enjoyed working with me....

I have never had an experience like the one I had at Schiffer. I have been at many similarly structured organizations: everything from other firms to a sorority to my school's law review. I have always been a well-liked, and more importantly, well-respected individual. Given all that I have told you, I truly feel that I was given no choice but to leave Schiffer, Mulligan.

Perhaps you or others think that I was overly sensitive or overly dramatic. However, I recommend considering how you would feel if all of this happened to your daughter day in and day out for their entire first year of practicing law. I know that every one of my law school friends, male and female, consistently wondered how I went to work every day.

I am sorry that the firm 'see[s] things differently.' As I mentioned to you, I tried to leave the firm with a 'no hard feelings' attitude which I hoped would be mutual and I'm truly confused as to why it was not. It seems terribly odd to me that Mike could engage in the behavior outlined above and be begged to stay at the firm, yet I was treated like a leper until the day I left.

I don't expect or particularly want a response from you. In addition, I do not intend to bad mouth Schiffer, Mulligan and I hope the courtesy will be reciprocal. I just wanted you to know how much your comment troubled me. This was a very sad year of my life and I'm glad it's over.

Sincerely,

Erin Gordon"

I did not hear back from Duncan after sending this letter — either in 1994 or 2023. A week after sending it in 2023, I followed up a second time. Again, he never responded.

This silence enraged and validated me. No matter how long ago the events were, Frederick failing to remember a 26-year-old woman crying in his office because of behavior by partners under his command was, in my opinion, inexcusable. When being reminded of it caused him to stop communicating with me altogether signaled to me that he grasped how egregious his — and the firm's — actions were.

THANE

Legal Assistant

A former college "mathlete" with a nerdy streak, Thane was a distinct favorite of The Club, though generally I found him to be a sweet guy.

Although, admittedly, we worked in different departments, I could never understand why Thane — a legal assistant who was in law school — was assigned tons of legal research and writing work when I, a full-blown associate, had none.

I was grateful for Thane's 2023 recollections, especially because, unlike Elizabeth or Frederick, he remembered me unequivocally. Thane's detailed reminiscences showed I'd made an impression on someone back then, that I was memorable.

What do you remember about Schiffer Mulligan during that time?

It was a special group of people who loved practicing law. There were elements that were dark — Frederick was one of those guys.

Ben was a very substantial mentor to me. He and Scott — they're really good people. It was really positive, really supportive. It was like a frat. There was definitely a frat mentality — lots of joking in the hallways, ribbing.

It was a different time. Women had to wear skirts and stockings. Men had to wear their jacket when walking around the office. Even on a Saturday it was business casual.

It was very male dominated, no question. Dixon Long represents that kind of male domination. Though it's changed dramatically in 30 years. By the time I left, women associates became the majority.

How do you view some of those frat-like conversations in 2023?

[A pause.] I don't remember it being mean-spirited or intended to harm people.

Over the years, [the women partners] didn't appreciate the frat aspect of the litigation group, but that's what made it really good. It just depends on how PC you want to be. Do you want people to be robotic and not joke around?

It could have made it hard for women to feel connected or that they belonged. It was hard to break into.

You have young adult daughters now. How would you feel if they were in that environment?

I raised them to be thick-skinned, to be able to deal with interactions of all kinds. As long as they were respected as women and given equal opportunities, I would be happy to have them in that environment.

What do you remember about me and Mike?

I was friends with Mike. He was bigger than life. I remember your relationship being a really good thing until it wasn't. It was soonish after the time of you moving to Chestnut. All of the sudden you were really close to him and he felt it was encroaching on his freedom. I remember it being a big deal when you were breaking up. It was very disruptive to the work environment. I remember him being teased, like, "What are you doing, you dumb ass, dating someone where you work?"

I'm a friend of the guy and I'm sure that I heard the version of the story that was skewed, that you were just a crazy wacko causing this, an emotional woman. But I understood at the time that it was a skewed story because I don't think I'd actually seen that from you.

[I recounted some of the incidents at the firm, including not being included in firm events, of having my photo defaced.]

It's really sad and unfortunate that you went through that. I have empathy. It's not right because it impacted you professionally.

It wasn't necessarily a woman thing — it was a power thing. When someone is rocking the boat, everyone closes ranks around it and encircles the problem. There was a lot of gaslighting.

It's too bad you didn't connect with Elizabeth during that time. She was a supporter of people in your position, women who had sex harassment claims. She was strident in her support of the victim and it hurt her career.

To me, our conversation in 2023 was pleasant and heartfelt. Thane and I reminisced with laughter, and at times, we were more somber. I found his recollections of me fair. Talking with him was in no way a battle.

Thane was one of the few interviewees who asked to see what I planned to use from our conversation. Per our agreement, once I had a working draft, I emailed him the partial transcript above. By way of introduction, I wrote:

"Hi Thane — Thank you again for speaking with me recently. It helped me both writing- and healing-wise. As promised, I'm reaching out to show you what I'd like to use from our conversation. For context, I've spoken to 13 people and everything you've said comports with what others have said. So with your permission. I'd like to use the following. Important note: the names are for my own drafting/your review purposes — I plan to change many actual names later. THANK YOU for your input. Erin"

To my surprise, I received this email three days later:

"Hi Erin — I have some issues with the way you have characterized many of my statements, and the fact that you left out a lot of what I had to say — which tends to emphasize the significance of the things you have chosen to include in a way that I do not believe is accurate. Did you record our conversation?"

Three minutes later, I replied:

"Hi Thane — I'm happy to discuss. I did not record our conversation but took copious notes. Let me know what you'd like me to add or take out to better reflect what you intended. As promised, I will not include anything that you don't want me to. I can also leave as is and change names/identifying information. Erin"

I received no response so three days later, I reached out again.

"Hi Thane — I'm checking back in on this. I definitely want to ensure you're comfortable. I can re-word, delete, adjust, add. I can change your name and identifying information. I can also show you my notes. (As you know, I've been a journalist for 25 years so I'm good at capturing conversations.) Please let me know what works for you. Thank you again for your help. Erin"

The next day, he wrote:

"Hi Erin — I will send you a more detailed email later this week. Thanks. Thane"

Within minutes, I wrote back:

"Great — I look forward to it. As I said, I want to make sure you're comfortable. If you're not, I can take out the interview altogether. Either way, I really appreciated our conversation. Erin"

I did not hear from Thane later that week or even later that month. About six weeks later, I reached out to him once again.

"Hi Thane — I'm following up on this. Please let me know how you'd like to proceed. Thanks! Erin"

I did not receive a reply. I emailed yet again about six weeks after that.

"Hi Thane — Hope your summer has been going great. I continue to work on this project and want to make sure you're comfortable with what's below. I've since changed your name and identifying information. Other additions/deletions you'd like? Erin"

I received no response, which, after so much pestering over so many months, including multiple offers to take out the interview altogether, I took as tacit permission to move forward.

TIM

Senior Associate

Tim Reids was Ben's deputy both work-wise and socially. He's the person who insisted that the misspellings on a summer associate applicant's resume could be overlooked because the law student was "very handsome."

I was grateful Tim, now about 60, agreed to speak with me. I was curious to ask, for example, why he arranged for Mike to attend that summer associate Tahoe trip two weeks *after* he'd left the firm knowing that I (who was at the firm serving as a summer associate mentor) would have attended otherwise. But about an hour before our scheduled video call, Tim sent this email:

"Hi Erin —

Unfortunately I am not going to be able to make our call today. I will reconnect to find a better time. Sorry for the late notice.

Best,

Tim"

Within minutes, I wrote back offering several alternative days and times to speak. I received no response.

A week later, I followed up with another email. As with Frederick Duncan after I sent a PDF of my departure letter, as with Thane after multiple attempts to confirm our conversation, I never heard from Tim again.

Given that The Club is still intact all these years later — whether by email or text, I don't know — I can only assume that Tim had heard about the topics of previous interviews for this project.

Chapter Twelve

2023

After the first few interviews with former colleagues and then finding old cards Mike had sent me (confirming that I had not imagined his initial enthusiasm for our romance), my dread in opening The File after nearly 30 years transformed into excitement. Discovering incidents I'd forgotten — Tim Reids's flippant email dismissing a handsome male applicant's resume error, Mike's overt threat to ruin my career — made me sick, but also renewed my commitment to re-examine my time in Big Law.

In fact, as my reporting proceeded, I grew consumed. Everything I saw and heard took on a potentially potent meaning. True to my sorting nature, I sought to uncover a new framework for that year's painful events. A monologue on TV, an expert quoted in a newspaper article, a friend's off-hand but sneakily wise observation about relationships — I sought to apply it all to my year at Schiffer Mulligan. The project was constantly on my mind. One of my Wordle rounds went from CLAIM to POWER to TOUGH.

The more I reported my own story, reliving the pain of that time, the more I began waking up in the middle of the night with my mind flying immediately back to 1993. I kept a small notebook by my bed for the insights that came to me in the way only a drowsy, middle-of-the-night thought can. I started growing sleepy during the day, whether from interrupted nighttime sleep or from the heaviness of the daily work on the book, including reaching out over and over to people who'd hurt me. In early 2023, the night after I typed up the final bits from The File and then wrote directly to Dixon Long, Jasper Brook, Frederick Duncan and others requesting their input for the book, I woke gasping from a nightmare about those same people murdering my family as a warning to stop writing.

The project shook up my brain like a snow globe. After every interview, the snowflakes would swirl around and around and it would take a day or two before they'd settle as I processed each source's recollections and insights and then realized that not a single person denied anything — not Frederick Duncan, not Elizabeth, not Max, Patrick or Thane.

I also felt a latent sadness hovering. I began to feel immense compassion for 24-year-old Erin. I realized how much the Schiffer Mulligan experience affected not just my career but, more importantly, my identity, something that should have been solidifying — rather than crumbling — in my mid-20's. Of course, everyone experiences failures and disappointments in life and in jobs. But what happened in 1993 cut right to what I felt about myself, how I defined myself. And despite accomplishments after Schiffer Mulligan, my self-esteem never recovered.

***

Friends who read early drafts of my story noted that I "still seem really bitter." But that's not accurate. Rather, I'm *newly* bitter. For the first time in 30 years, I'm shifting blame *from myself*. For the first time, I'm seeing that I'd long *adopted* the firm's, The Club's view of me.

One friend suggested I give The Club and others "the middle finger and show them all the wonderful things about your life despite what they did to you." But recovering from the effects of gaslighting is not, for me anyway, an instantaneous process. Although I am proud of my family, my subsequent Stanford degree, my marathon medal, the volunteer work I do, I still feel worthless much of the time. The self-doubt, the low self-esteem hit me at a critical inflection point in my life, my most vulnerable moment professionally. I see the combustible way events unfolded, and I am committed to the personal work I must now do to reverse the effects.

This project spotlighted how negativity bias creeps into the stories we tell ourselves about who we are. Studies show that for most people, negative events or feelings have a far more significant impact on our emotional state than positive events even when they're of equal proportion. What I uncovered in The File and heard from sources contrasted with my memory of being annoying or clingy. But my belief in my own "weak" behavior had caused me so much shame, akin to Kelli, who spent decades guilt-ridden that she'd had, as a 14-year-old, an affair with a married man three times her age.

I also began to turn self-judgment into compassion. I understand now that being devastated was nothing to be ashamed of. I had *every right* to be given how Mike, The Club and Schiffer Mulligan treated me. There should have been no shame in being brokenhearted. All it showed was that I'd been trusting and eager to love.

Some might see this story as a cautionary tale for young women entering the workforce. But I see now that I actually did everything a lowly first-year attorney could to change the situation and still nothing improved. The more apt lesson is for anyone who's been unfair to themselves in the stories they tell. Like what Kelli had long been telling herself, the narrative *I'd* stuck to didn't reflect reality. I'd misplaced my anger and other negative emotions — towards myself.

***

Reporting this story also allowed me to begin disentangling my self-worth from my utter insignificance in the power structure I'd been up against. I finally understand that I was inconsequential in a system that was set up precisely to keep me inconsequential. Associates really are fungible billing units, particularly if they don't mirror the demographics of the partnership. My eager, inspired efforts to start my rainmaking path as a first-year associate, which I believed would help me stand out, especially given my pathetic lack of actual legal work, would *of course* be ignored. A first-year associate is a cog in a wheel, meant to do grunt work to make money for partners, who would never cede business generation credit to a brand-new lawyer. While I cannot prove it, I do believe, though, that my efforts might have been at least *noted* had I been a male associate.

Over the years, I've had people insist that I was "just a pawn" caught up in a political clash between labor group head Jasper Brook and managing partner Frederick Duncan.

But I wasn't "just" anything. I was a person.

Others affiliated with the firm have suggested that my now being happily married with kids should make up for all that happened so long ago at Schiffer Mulligan.

Kelli is happily married with kids. Does that make up for her being sexually abused as a teenager?

Others have suggested that I write this book purely as personal therapy and then put it in a drawer so as not to harm others' careers.

Still others, who know nothing about my job satisfaction or income, insist the events aren't worth rehashing because I successfully pivoted to another career, one that I'm good at.

Those dismissive comments fill me with an impotent rage and hammer home how desensitized powerful individuals are to the life-altering effects of misogyny, gaslighting and workplace bullying. The individuals who minimized my lived experience were — and continue to be — unconcerned with my humanity. It showed how little a young woman at the firm mattered then — and now.

The pain was compounded by the fact that several sources didn't even remember me. Of course, I understand that I was only at the firm for a year (plus the summer before) way back in 1993. Even my few friends at the firm began interviews with statements like, "Gosh, that was so long ago." And of course it's human nature that most peoples' memories center around themselves, around incidents and emotions that directly impacted them.

But given that once I raised the hostile work environment issues with management, a labor partner flew to San Francisco to conduct an "investigation" and days later the firm's entire employment policy shifted to require mandatory arbitration agreements, I am stunned that people in power had absolutely no recollection of that — or of me at all. I deliberately conducted every interview via video so that former colleagues could see my face in case it helped refresh their memories. More than one individual confessed that I didn't even look familiar.

Troubled, I asked my therapist how this could possibly be. But she was unsurprised that I'd been forgotten. "You — and what you raised then and now — don't comport with their belief in themselves as good people," she explained, "so you were easily and conveniently dropped from their cognition."

My conversation with pretty boy Max had a particularly upsetting moment. When he was naming others, besides himself, who were in The Club, he mentioned Mike. Then he paused, looked skyward and then said, "Wait, you dated Mike, didn't you?"

What?!

How could my relationship be so worthy of being gossiped about and disparaged over beers in 1993 and yet also so insignificant as to be barely remembered in 2023?

How could something that impacted my life so profoundly be a complete afterthought to this guy who'd been in The Club, who'd been party to many of those inappropriate conversations?

At that point in my reporting, emotions shifted to rage, and a sudden urgency took hold. I ramped up my work because I wanted all of the offenders — many, like Jasper Brook, Frederick Duncan and Dixon Long, in their 80's now — to read my story. I wanted lawyers I worked with at Schiffer Mulligan and then at my next firm to see *why* I wasn't such a great lawyer and what just a little nurturing — rather than derision — might have done.

As I continued reporting, I learned that some of the men at Schiffer Mulligan were also subject to Big Law's hierarchical system. Some didn't make partner the first go-around. Some were emasculated by more powerful partners. Some were subject to internal, even vicious machinations regarding business generation credit. All had their own billable hour and client development pressures.

Many of the bullies were bullied themselves.

They were just higher on the Big Law pyramid.

***

Because I'm a writer, friends often ask what I'm working on. I slowly began to share with close friends the details of this project. This was a big deal because I'd held the story so close for three decades, afraid of how I'd be perceived. While I often joked that I shifted to journalism because I'd been the "world's worst lawyer," I never shared what really happened at Schiffer Mulligan — or later. Even my husband knew only the barest of details.

A couple of months after starting work on this story, I was on a girls weekend with several close friends. In response to the question of what I was working on, I said, "A memoir of my first year in law." I paused, then added, "It was kind of traumatic." They prodded for details, so I began to share. I spoke for almost 25 minutes straight, spurred on, heartened and validated by their facial expressions — brows furrowed in sympathetic pain and jaws dropping with each detail.

Yet it wasn't all unfettered support for the project. My mother worried how I'd come across in this story, fueling my insecurities. My parents begged me repeatedly not to use real names, and I lost so much sleep agonizing over that decision. I also began having nightmares: of being chased, of insect infestations, of being vomited on.

But I leaned into it. In my effort to uncover how much of what happened was at-tributable to me, how much was my own fault, I implored every source to be brutally honest in their recollections and their descriptions of me. I braced myself for adjectives like "annoying, immature, naive" or at the very least "too sensitive." I even prompted them, offering those very adjectives as suggestions, letting sources know that I could take it. I expected to hear examples of how I'd been, as Mike termed me, a basket case. Instead, I heard "eager," "nice" and "smart."

***

During the weeks I interviewed former colleagues, I had a dream about my cat Mensch, something that happens about once a month. But this time, it was more than a dream. I actually *felt* the weight of him on my left shoulder, where he'd nestle whenever I slept on my back. A week later, I was at my chiropractor, a petite and magical Mexican woman named Margarita who'd helped me with everything from neck pain to hot flashes. As she worked, I lay on my back. She paused and then said offhandedly, "Do you have a cat? Or do you like cats?"

"I used to have a cat who was, like, the love of my life. And I volunteer at the SPCA by socializing cats."

"Makes sense," Margarita said, "because there's a cat here."

"Really?" I asked, skeptical but intrigued given the intense dream I'd had just the week before.

"Yes. I see that he's all grey."

He.

All Grey.

"Wow. My cat was a male. And that's exactly what he looked like."

"Well," she continued, "Mitchy wants you to know he's here with you."

"What did you call him?"

"I'm hearing 'Mitchy.'"

Oh my God.

"His name was Mensch," I said. "I called him Mensch-y."

I'd never mentioned Mensch to Margarita. I'd never written about him either — the way I felt about him wasn't something she could have Googled. I'm an atheist who has little faith in the existence of things I can't see, even radio waves. But she said what she said, and I was gobsmacked.

What could I do but take it as some sort of sign? Mensch was the focal point of my affections for many years, *particularly* in 1993 when I was so distraught. I decided Margarita's insight was a signal that, despite the pain accompanying it, my intense writing project was on the right path.

Still, not infrequently, I'd think, "Why am I doing this? Readers aren't going to care how deeply this ostracizing at Schiffer Mulligan affected me. They'll say, 'Why didn't she just move on or grow a fucking *backbone*?'" But then I'd come across some tidbit, like a new scientific study by Tulane University researchers, published in *Current Biology*, that discovered that social rank — particularly in females — affects the stress response. Psychosocial stress is unequivocally impacted by social instability, according to the study. Perhaps, I reasoned, other women might relate to what I experienced and somehow benefit from hearing my story.

I plowed forward.

***

If I didn't hear back from a potential source, I waited anywhere from a couple of weeks to a couple of months and then tried again, giving everyone two opportunities to respond in case the first email or postal letter was lost or forgotten. Reaching out to sources whom I expected to be reluctant (Jasper Brook, Dixon Long, Ben Bucknell, Tim Reids and David Powell) filled me with a sick kind of glee. *I'm writing a book, motherfuckers.*

I buffeted the follow-ups by mentioning that I'd already interviewed more than a dozen individuals, including partners, associates and experts in hostile work environments and workplace bullying (signaling, more directly this time, the focus of the book), and had also preserved a long paper trail of primary sources, including emails and memos from 1993 (signaling that their own past communications might be included). This book and those messages serve as a secondary, 2023 paper trail.

In sending follow-up interview requests, glee was replaced by a heaviness. Yes, I still wanted those sources to quake in their boots. After all, their actions changed my whole life. But I didn't want to threaten anyone's professional reputations even though they'd destroyed mine. I chose to move forward, drawing on Anne Lamott's words in her book *Bird by Bird*: "You own everything that happened to you. Tell your stories. If people wanted you to write warmly about them, they should have behaved better."

***

In the past, when I've written novels, I'm single-minded and diligent, sticking to a strict scene-by-scene writing schedule. In February, for example, I can tell you exactly what day in May I'll be working on Scene 32. But in working on *this* project, the first about my own life, I dreaded writing in a way I never had before. I started drafting only after I'd outlined the shit out of the book and had no choice but to move forward with writing or abandon it altogether.

For every other book, I approached the story chronologically, starting with chapter one and moving forward. But for this book, I started by first writing what comes *after* the law, because that's when things started to turn around in my life and that's all I could face in the beginning. I had to ease into the worst of it.

***

"Oh, wow," my husband said one night as I was partway through the first draft. He was scanning the U.S. Postal Service email that previews the next day's snail mail. "You have a letter coming tomorrow from Schiffer Mulligan."

"Really?" I said.

"What could it be?" we wondered.

"A cease-and-desist letter?" my husband speculated.

"They can't stop me from writing a book," I insisted. "Was it from the San Francisco or Los Angeles office?"

My husband used his finger tips to expand the image of the letter on its way.

The San Diego office. Huh.

The next day, I waited for the mail with the nervous eagerness of a second-semester high school senior in the 1980's waiting for college admissions decisions.

When I opened the envelope, I pulled out a card that read, "We've Missed You!" It was from Schiffer Mulligan's Attorney Alumni Program, inviting me to sign up for alumni newsletters and reunions.

Um, maybe keep track of the associates who almost sued you for harassment.

***

Something that ate at me as I reported and wrote was how this book would be perceived by a mainstream audience. I kept envisioning 1-star reviews, many of which I imagined beginning with "Why didn't she just...?" akin to critics who'd said about kidnapping victim Elizabeth Smart, "Why didn't she just scream when that crazy couple had her out in the real world?" (And another 1-star review for comparing myself to a kidnap and rape victim.) Or akin to clueless, insensitive people who questioned why Jennifer Newsom faked an orgasm as Harvey Weinstein allegedly raped her.

One star: *Why didn't she just stand up for herself?* (I tried. No one listened.)

One star: *Why didn't she just move on? I mean, the guy was clearly an asshole.* (I know that now.)

One star: *This middle-aged mom needs to get a life. She's whining about something that happened three decades ago.*

One star: *Boo hoo. People at your fancy law firm weren't nice to you. On a scale of rainbows to the Holocaust, this doesn't even rate.*

One star: *Cry me a river. Women have been second-class citizens since Eve. How could she have been so foolish to expect anything different?*

One star: *She must have had an inflated opinion of herself to presume that the firm would do anything other than protect the institution at the expense of the individual.*

I imagined 1-star reviews for complaining about harassment in my high paid, elite job, like Gwyneth Paltrow's I-missed-a-day-of-skiing complaint. After all, as awful as it was, I was lucky just to *get* a prestigious job at Schiffer Mulligan.

Comparing trauma was a contest I didn't want to enter.

I feared derision, being made fun of.

Then I read a line from the book *Maame* by Jessica George, which prompted me, once again, to trudge forward despite fears: "A person's troubles are not measured by the size of those troubles, but by how much they weigh on the individual carrying them."

Chapter Thirteen

2023

In my quest to gather expert opinions about my Schiffer Mulligan experience, I reached out to several authorities in gender and the law, hostile work environments, and workplace bullying. As a journalist, I wanted neutral, expert input, not merely confirmation of my feelings. I sought to place my experience in the context of women in the law generally.

I first interviewed Joan Williams, founding director of the Center for WorkLife Law at UC College of the Law, an advocacy and research organization focused on racial, gender and class equity. Williams explained that the "long hours culture" of Big Law emerged at precisely the same time that women were flooding into higher education. That ended up wiping out advantages that women might have gained and instead preserved male dominance in the legal profession, something that men, of course, were deeply invested in. In other words, consciously or unconsciously, this "grinder" mentality was men dictating the terms, a way for them to mark territory, a way to ensure the profession was unwelcoming and harder for women to navigate.

According to Williams, decades earlier, many white-collar men actually prided themselves on keeping "banker's hours" of merely 11 - 3 and then going to play golf. But as soon as women began entering elite professions, our culture changed the definition of the ideal worker, normalizing the "work devotion schema." Not surprisingly, the legal profession "embraced it gleefully," Williams said. "After all, the more that associates worked, the richer the partners got."

At the same time, in the '80's, an increasing income inequality emerged between law firm partners and government lawyers. "It became an order of magnitude more" as profits per partner shot up at private firms, Williams said, adding with a chuckle, "Are we really talking about salaries and hours here? I don't think so."

Joyce Sterling, a law professor at the University of Denver, similarly noted that, "By 1993, we thought big changes had taken place in the legal profession. Women were being hired at firms at entry level at least close to parity with men. We thought, 'Gender won't be a problem in ten years.' But it turned out those women were not promoted at the same rate as men."

I spoke to Sterling along with her longtime collaborator Bryant Garth, a professor of law at the University of California, Irvine and co-director of UCI's Center for Empirical Research on the Legal Profession. In their research for *After the JD: The First Results of a National Study of Legal Careers*, a joint publication of the American Bar Association and the National Association of Law Placement Foundation for Law Career Research and Education, Sterling and Garth heard "so many stories" about the dominant male culture in law, "about women who don't support other women, about women forced to make a choice between the firm or their family. No one was supporting them, and they lost their commitment."

A key objective criterion for success as a law firm lawyer is hours billed. Partners give assignments to associates, which is how associates meet their billable hour requirements. It's the partners in charge — the majority of whom were men — who controlled that.

I discovered for myself within days of starting work at Schiffer Mulligan that Big Law was not always a meritocracy. Every new lawyer still needed someone to pick them and bring them along, preserving the male dominance because men often pick other men to mentor. The vast majority of men in power then were straight and white. I can only imagine how challenging it must have been to be a person of color or openly queer as a Big Law associate back then.

Even women partners, I found during my own interviews, still felt they had to prove themselves to their male counterparts, leaving them little energy or interest in taking new female associates under their wings. It was maddening to me at the time. Later, I understood that it was another example of how far behind women really were in Big Law. Any empirical statistics showing that women were finally *in* the profession told an incomplete story.

Garth confirmed that a critical element of any law firm lawyer's professional advancement is having a mentor. "You need to be adopted by someone, usually a male. And it can't just be any mentor. The mentor needs to be in the power structure, and in law firms, if you have clients, you have power. It's easier for men to find those mentor relationships in part because there's a positive bias for the work that men do."

In contrast, there's often no "buddy system" for women. They often leave even when they're doing well because, without a mentor, no one tells them they're doing well.

One of the women Garth and Sterling interviewed said that every year she identified what she needed to learn to progress and then identified a partner at her large firm who could teach her each of those skills. But it was a Catch-22, Garth added. "How assertive can you be? The men could swear, for example, but when women would swear or be aggressive, it could be deemed inappropriate" by the clients or partnership.

As a new lawyer in 1993, I naively thought that we were past all that, that women's growing presence in law firm life proved that historical inequities — and gender-based harassment — didn't exist. From my very first days in Big Law, I knew that was wrong.

***

Preparing for my interview with longtime labor and employment expert Patricia Gillette, I expected her to be a champion of this project, a supporter of my story. But to my surprise, she disputed the premise from the get-go, suggesting that I was "late to the party" by writing about a hostile work environment I experienced in the early 1990's. She insisted that my story was "nothing new and different."

My experience at Schiffer Mulligan, Gillette said, was "not an indication of all law firms." Though she did concede that industry culture does favor men and that even the women in Big Law could behave like "queen bees," meaning they may not be automatically or unquestioningly supportive of young female associates coming up through the ranks.

Gillette insisted, though, that any female lawyer will be treated equally as men as long as she has her own business. Power, she said, is driven by who controls the money. "I was a rainmaker," she said of her experience in Big Law. "I was on every leadership team."

With each passing minute that Gillette spoke during our interview, my resolve to continue with this project shrank.

Didn't I try to bring in business as a first-year associate? Maybe no one will care about this book, just like no one cared back then about what was happening.

Who wants to read about shit that happened 30 years ago?

Maybe it wasn't the firm culture or the profession but me?

Despite labeling herself an optimist and suggesting that my story was tired, Gillette conceded that the profession still has a way to go. Specifically, in "Women Are Ready: Is the Legal Industry?", an article on her website, Gillette wrote, "[T]he obstacles for women ascending into positions of power are systemic, requiring an overhaul of the way we think about how we practice law and reward attorneys in our firms."

According to Gillette, areas for overhaul include: succession planning (lucrative client relationships have long been controlled by white men and then passed onto white men); diverse pitch teams (efforts to bring in women and minorities to client pitch meetings must be real and not merely "for appearances"); origination credit (when men get out-sized financial rewards, often assigned for life, for bringing in clients even when others, including women, actually do the work and maintain the positive client relationships, it's a recipe for selfish maneuvers and bad behavior); and monitoring (law firms should monitor what impacts professional growth, such as how well or poorly women assimilate back into work after parental leave).

I was surprised and disappointed that Gillette rejected the premise of my project. She told me, "You seem really smart" and suggested I write a different kind of book altogether. It was one of the many times I considered abandoning this project that was depleting my emotional energy and taking time away from possibly more lucrative journalism work. But whenever friends asked what I was working on and I told them, they chimed in with their own stories of workplace harassment or bullying. And readers of my various drafts would insist, "This story needs to get out there."

Back in 1993, when I felt so isolated and misunderstood, I would have given anything to discover that there were psychological terms for the behavior I was being subjected to. It would have meant everything to read a story like this. So I re-gathered my resolve.

For as many women who've had positive experiences in Big Law like Gillette, there are likely at least the same number of women — in and out of the legal profession — who've experienced a hostile work environment and workplace bullying. After all, although there are many women who've been blackout drunk who were not then assaulted like Chanel Miller, there are many, many who were. My story included a toxic confluence of people and events — a bad relationship with a colleague, a clubby environment. But whenever I told female lawyer friends about this project, many would jump in with harrowing examples of their own — a stapler thrown, a breast groped.

After reading a draft of this manuscript, one lawyer friend wrote, "In our twenties, we felt so adult, so independent, so in control of our destinies. Looking back from this vantage point, we were so, so young. We were young attorneys before there was any meaningful change."

And it's questionable whether meaningful change really has occurred. After my conversation with Gillette, I spoke to Susan Strauss, a Minnesota-based workplace bullying consultant. She confirmed that the kind of behavior I experienced in 1993 is "alive and well. There's still a patriarchy, still toxic masculinity, still power differentials," she said. "You even have women bullying other women."

Still.

In interviewing Strauss, I was trying to determine if I experienced workplace bullying or "simply" a hostile work environment. When I asked Strauss to define workplace bullying, she said, "Therein lies the problem. There's no law against it and it means different things to different people. The definition is up for grabs." Generally, though, workplace bullying includes behaviors that violate the employer's own code of conduct, defined in their policies, and the concept need not be related to a protected class like gender, age or race so it offers broader protection for the victim. "It's behavior that's rude, obnoxious, disrespectful, intimidating, and intended to demean an individual."

Law firms tend to regard bullying victims as people who can't take a joke, Strauss noted. "Lawyers are intelligent and ego-driven. They feel an entitlement because of the work they're doing, their power and knowledge base."

When I asked if my picture being defaced would properly be characterized as workplace bullying, she said, "They wouldn't have done it to a male colleague. It was rude, disrespectful and intended to intimidate you and put you in your place."

The primary problem in coaching lawyers in workplace bullying, Strauss added, is this: "If you've got an attorney with a lot of billable hours who's a real jerk, the partners don't want to come down on him because he brings in the money. High achievers who bring in money are not held accountable. They're entitled, privileged, and get away with it. It's a dilemma."

Still.

Cheryl Strayed wrote *Wild*, an account of her solo hike along the Pacific Crest Trail, many years after she'd completed the trek. The details — the flora and fauna — may have changed in the time between her hike and when she wrote the book. But the Pacific Crest Trail itself is still there.

My story, I concluded, is still relevant.

Chapter Fourteen

2023

Although much has improved at law firms in the last 30 years, there are still problems.

"Firms don't do enough self-reflection," according to Joyce Sterling, the University of Denver law professor whose decades of research focuses on women in law. "They think they're doing better, but our surveys show that men say firms are 'giving women all the opportunities to succeed' and women say just the opposite." With some frequency, women often make partner in name only, maintaining non-equity status, and many leave when they realize that all of their hard work goes towards "enriching these guys," Sterling adds.

When I told Sterling and her collaborator, UC Irvine law professor Bryant Garth, about having experienced a hostile work environment with absolutely no repercussions for the offenders, Sterling said that kind of result is "still very true" today. Anyone with power — in law firms, that's any rainmaker who contributes mightily to the economic pie, of which all of the other partners partake — "is still kind of above the law."

The Clarence Thomas hearings showed that an attorney could be called out for harassment but then what followed was to demonize the woman without any consequences to the man, according to Joan Williams, the professor at UC College of the Law. "It perpetuated the stereotype of a vengeful lying slut and showed women what happened if you brought it up. It was like, 'What was it about *you* that made him come onto you?'" Another common trope is that only humorless, difficult women call men out, said Williams, who herself has been referred to in writings as a "feminazi."

Certainly, the #metoo movement helped the demands for accountability and it became less costly for women to say that harassment has happened, particularly because social media proved that it happens to most women, Williams added. Also, "feminism grinds day after day so we have 30 years more headway than we did in 1993."

And yet...

Even though Christine Blasey Ford testified — credibly, in my opinion — before the Senate Judiciary Committee in 2018 about not just being harassed but actually *assaulted* by Brett Kavanaugh, he is now serving as a US Supreme Court Justice alongside Clarence Thomas.

***

During my year at Schiffer Mulligan — when I had untold hours to read given that I was given hardly any work — I devoured feminist classics, including Erica Jong's *Fear of Flying* and Betty Friedan's *The Feminist Mystique*. But it was Susan Faludi's *Backlash: The Undeclared War Against America's Women*, that affected me most. Published in 1991, *Backlash* described how the alleged "costs" of women's professional gains in the 1970's — including an infertility epidemic — were false assertions driven by the Reagan-era media and popular culture.

I loved *Backlash*. It inspired me to keep writing — and to take action. Looking back, my version of "taking action" was ridiculous. I felt like Wonder Woman after writing a letter to a car company critiquing its TV commercial that declared men should buy a particular car model because "Women dig it!"

But I also wrote directly to Faludi, to tell her how much the book meant to me. I recently found in a file (not The File) a typewritten letter back to me, dated January 8, 1994. Faludi wrote:

"Thank you so much for your kind and thoughtful letter. I'm pleased — and honored — that *Backlash* has made a difference for you. It means a great deal to me to know that my book has reached readers such as yourself.

I'm glad to hear that you intend to focus your pro bono work on women's causes, and that you've decided to write about your own experiences. It's been wonderful to see so many women in the last year converting their feelings of isolation and 'craziness' into constructive anger.

I hope you'll keep speaking out and expressing your thoughts. I appreciate your taking the time to express them to me.

Sincerely yours,

Susan Faludi"

This letter came decades before DMs and websites made it easier to connect with authors, or anyone we look up to. I was buoyed by this lovely, personal response from Faludi. It was validating even though I realize now I wasn't doing nearly enough to promote women's rights.

I thought I'd become empowered just by *becoming* a young, female lawyer.

I naively thought that threatening not to buy a car because "Women dig it!" might influence corporate strategy.

I thought that writing an internal memo to Frederick Duncan, Jasper Brook and Dixon Long, after Long's sham investigation, demanding that "I want to work as little as possible with Jasper Brook and I do not want him evaluating my work in the formal review process" meant that I was a feminist warrior.

I thought that by saying "because I wasn't treated well" in my exit interview with a clueless Schiffer Mulligan administrator asking why I was leaving meant that I was becoming forthright and growing more comfortable speaking my piece.

I thought that by simply reading those feminist bibles, I truly grasped what was happening at the firm, in Big Law and in the culture at large.

While tempting, I'm not criticizing myself and my naiveté. Rather, I'm criticizing society, the system.

It was all an illusion that women were equal.

It's taken nearly 30 years for me to understand why no one listened when I pounded my proverbial fists and screamed that what was happening wasn't right, to understand that no matter what I did, I still lacked something critical, something that remained elusive.

Power.

Chapter Fifteen

2023

For several years pre-pandemic, I volunteered in public high schools teaching yoga to teenagers. Every semester I included a lesson on power posing. I spent a few minutes explaining Harvard professor Amy Cuddy's research indicating that bringing one's body into expansive, powerful postures for a few minutes before important events can bolster confidence and performance. Then I'd guide them through triangle, warrior 3 and similar big-body postures. My idea was not only to boost students' confidence but to give them actual practice taking up physical space, to experience what it felt like to embody their whole selves.

The truth is, I was primarily teaching the girls in the class because power is still deeply affected by gender dynamics — and double standards. Instead of telling girls they shouldn't get blackout drunk, we should tell boys not to rape women. Patrick, one of the Schiffer Mulligan associates who was friends with Mike, noted during our 2023 video call that it had been risky for me to date someone I worked with. Yet *he'd* married a woman who worked as a secretary at the firm.

Even though I had to do courage meditations and felt compelled to put on makeup before many of the interviews for this book, I knew these people no longer had any *power* over me. They could no longer affect my career. It's why the mere act of sending an email to Jasper Brook and certain members of The Club about the book I was writing made me feel powerful. No longer feeling ashamed or intimidated into *not* telling my story was a meaningful step into my untapped strength.

And power is, perhaps, what motivated Mike to badmouth me the summer I took the bar exam, just months before I was to join the same firm as a first-year associate. "I bet he was scared, afraid you'd show him up once you arrived at the firm," one of my closest friends said when I confided in her about what had happened that year, about my textbook "degradation ceremony." Again, power had been mine to strive for but his to lose.

Chapter Sixteen

1994

In 1994, it was extremely uncommon for associates to leave a law firm after a single year. The earliest acceptable time to "lateral" to another firm was in the third or fourth year. In those days, looking for another law firm job before then raised red flags. Considerations like culture fit, gig economies, remote work, corporate responsibility and workplace well-being were not in the cultural vocabulary and certainly not in the law firm milieu. My husband was at his "first firm" for nearly 27 years.

But through a family connection, I was lucky enough to get an interview at Thelen, Marrin, Johnson & Bridges, a San Francisco-based firm that was just starting to bounce back after bleeding lawyers, many of whom had gone to...wait for it...Schiffer Mulligan. (Reggie and Irv had been part of the environmental group that had once been at Thelen.) I believe that was part of the appeal in interviewing me, an extremely junior lawyer finishing only her first year. In fact, during my interview with Thelen's managing partner, he explicitly said, "Nice to see the train coming the other way."

As at Schiffer Mulligan, the labor and employment group at Thelen was quite busy so I marketed myself as a labor lawyer since, thanks to managing partner Frederick Duncan's unilateral reassignment, I technically was. I remember Linus, co-head of Thelen's labor group, asking me during the interview if I'd done wage and hour work. I answered "no," but didn't reveal that actually I had no idea what wage and hour work was. There were hints during interviews with Thelen's various labor lawyers that there was no love lost between Linus and Jim, co-heads of the department. I. Did. Not. Care. Nothing, I figured, could be as damaging to me personally as what had taken place at Schiffer Mulligan.

I received an offer from Thelen the day after my interview and I accepted on the spot. I didn't even mind that the salary was slightly lower than what I'd been making at Schiffer Mulligan, a downward trend in my annual income that continues to this day. All I knew was that I was finally getting *out*.

In contrast to the huge after-hours party that Schiffer Mulligan threw for Mike when he left, my departure meal was lunch with a grand total of two friends. When I said goodbye to Ben on that last day, *he conceded to my face* that I'd started at Schiffer Mulligan "0 for 2."

I once saw an interview with Cindy Crawford when she was married to Richard Gere. The interviewer asked how she dealt with rumors and lies about her and their marriage. She said that Gere had taught her "you know your own truth." While I understood that concept theoretically, I found it close to impossible to apply to my own life given that dozens of powerful men insisted that I had not, in fact, experienced a hostile work environment. I left Schiffer Mulligan not triumphant but deeply wounded, questioning my judgment, my voice, my truth.

I negotiated a start date at Thelen two or three weeks out. During that time off, I spent time reading in bed with Mensch purring at my side and spent one night at a small bed and breakfast in Napa. While there, I went to a nearby spa, something that seemed like a person should do to decompress from a year like I'd had. There, I soaked in some weird mineral bath trying to relax but instead sat there wondering how I "should be" feeling. I was lonely and confused.

A number of studies indicate that the effect of trauma may depend on an individual's age at the time of the event. That is, people are especially vulnerable at certain critical points in life, particularly childhood, adolescence and young adulthood. For example, the emotional impact of losing a parent at age five is different than at 35.

Traumas that occur during young adulthood strongly impact identity formation and are likely to have an outsized impact. I now see why being beaten down at my first professional job profoundly damaged my sense of self. With my 30-year vantage point, I also see that what happened at Schiffer Mulligan dramatically impacted what happened next, at Thelen.

***

Thelen's offices were at Two Embarcadero, a neighboring building to Schiffer Mulligan in the Embarcadero Center. I still saw those same circular floor tiles, still rode those exterior escalators. Whereas Schiffer was all pale blues and light wood, Thelen's offices were decorated in dark wood and hunter green. On my first day I wore a plain, single-colored suit (!). Despite my couple of weeks off, as I waited in the reception area, I felt bone tired. Utterly drained. When the HR administrator came out to meet me, I plastered on a smile and thought, "I don't know if I can do this all over again."

I realize now that I wanted out from Schiffer Mulligan but I didn't really want "in" at Thelen. And looking back, I had no hope of succeeding at Thelen. While I admitted during my interview with Linus that I didn't have wage and hour experience, I was too full of shame to reveal to anyone there that I didn't really have *any* experience. Thelen thought it was hiring a second-year associate. In fact, I'd had a year of backward professional growth, doing little more than drafting a few insignificant memos and following orders from partners to execute administrative tasks.

Given that Linus and Jim, the co-heads of Thelen's labor group, reportedly hated each other, I didn't want to get caught in the middle of another pissing match like the one between Frederick Duncan and Jasper Brook that culminated in the Brook memo. But I didn't know who I could trust at Thelen. Even if I did confide my lack of practical experience in a Thelen partner, even offering to start over as a first-year associate with a first-year's salary, would they call over to professional colleagues at Schiffer Mulligan to find out why I left so soon after starting there? Would they hear I was "trouble" and rescind my offer?

I hoped that I'd finally get substantive work at Thelen.

I hoped that I'd be mentored by a partner or senior associate.

I hoped that my legal career would finally have a successful — if belated — lift-off.

Thelen's culture was better than Schiffer Mulligan's but unpleasant in its own way.

For instance, labor partner Mick Malley often demanded that I follow him downstairs and outside so that he could smoke while giving me an assignment. This required me to take notes while balancing on one foot — in a skirt — so I could rest a legal pad on a lifted knee while he casually leaned against the side of the building and puffed away. Malley was among my biggest critics and wrote in one of my reviews that he wouldn't feel comfortable giving me anything beyond an assignment meant for a legal assistant. (One friend, who happened to be Malley's partner at their previous firm, recalled recently,

"Mick was a difficult guy who was full of himself.") One former client I spoke to in 2023 told me Malley "wasn't the brightest bulb."

When Oprah asked Michelle Obama how she handled feeling intimidated while seated at large tables among smart, powerful men, Michelle replied, "You realize pretty quickly that a lot of them aren't that smart." At both firms, I had an inkling this was true. But I didn't trust my instincts and allowed myself to be cowed by partners like Malley, who I found inconsiderate and kind of repulsive.

As a Thelen associate, I flew to Orange County several times for court appearances on some case that I can no longer remember. The appearances were typically scheduled for 9 a.m., which required flying down the night before and staying in a hotel. I hated being away from Mensch and the whole rigmarole seemed so *wasteful*. (These days, of course, those kinds of low-level appearances can be made by phone or video call, which is far more practical and cost-effective.) Once, I arrived at the Orange County courtroom to learn that the judge had the afternoon before issued a ruling in our favor, so no appearance had even been necessary. But the clerk hadn't bothered to notify us, which cost the client thousands of dollars in my unnecessary travel. Another time I arrived home from one of those Orange County trips in the evening and took a cab from the airport directly to my apartment. I called Jim, the partner, to update him on what we needed to do next. He asked if I'd done it yet, implying that I should have gone straight from the airport to the office. "You gotta get *on* this stuff," he said in a chiding dad tone. Even though nothing could really be *done* at that time of night, it was an unwelcome reminder that I just couldn't muster the killer drive that clients expect their litigators to have.

In my second year at Thelen, I attended a firm-wide labor group retreat in Southern California. At one point, we sat in a hotel conference room around a huge oval table as partners presented slideshows on topics like client development and the group's economics. About 45 minutes in, I had what can best be described as an out-of-body experience. Suddenly, I saw the meeting from above my own eye level. I panned around to the lawyers seated at the table — the arrogant divorcees, the self-important creeps, the uninteresting workaholics, the associates prematurely aging from stress. I saw that their influence — in general and over me, in particular — was outsized compared to their manners, their intelligence, their kindness. I would *never* choose to be friends with these people in any other setting.

I realized with a sudden clarity that zapped the breath from me: *I don't want to be anything like these people.*

To be sure, I did meet some wonderful people at Thelen (primarily outside the labor group) who are still friends today, including one who years later introduced me to my husband. Overall, though, I spent more energy on teaching writing classes at Hastings law school part-time and taking writing classes myself than I did trying to salvage my nascent legal career. I was drawn far more to activities that played to my strengths. All of that was reflected in my performance reviews at Thelen.

In December 1994, a few months after I started, labor department co-chair Jim Garter wrote:

"Writing is her strong suit."

"Has had an opportunity to relate to 2 clients and did well."

[Regarding client development,] "This is Erin's strong suit. Goes out of her way to ingratiate herself with clients. Good social skills... Erin has all of the skills to be a rainmaker." "Goes out of her way to interact socially and professionally with clients."

"Erin does take initiative in dealing with opposing counsel, clients, etc. However, completing legal tasks, anticipating what needs to be done to get a project finished, needs work. Erin is willing to work hard but needs to take a more proactive approach to assignments."

"Her pleasant personality makes it a joy to work with her and clients welcome her. However, Erin's lack of thoroughness in legal projects and her willingness to present a less than completed project as final have caused concern."

Gil wrote, "[S]he can be relied upon to find pertinent cases, analyze them correctly and be timely in responding to assignments."

In April 1995, partner Jan Bent, a spacey redhead who was allegedly a killer trial lawyer, though I could never picture it, drafted a memo to the head of the labor department that I wasn't told about until many months later: "My concern is that Erin is not thorough, does not think through the questions, brings me half an answer, and then brings me the wrong answer. There is really no excuse for this behavior." She described another example and concluded, "Again she brought me a project that was half done, and the half that had been done was not done correctly. I would like to have this memo put in her file and considered with her upcoming review."

As rotten as a few of these reviews were, not one person questioned my "interpersonal" skills as Jasper Brook had. In fact, I believe I was kept on far longer than I should have been precisely because I was well-liked.

I don't argue that my work at Thelen was strong. The partners were assigning me second-year work when I'd spent my first year at Schiffer Mulligan with almost no assignments. Looking back, I'm aggravated, though, that no partner cared enough to help me.

How did writing memos behind my back for "my file" help anyone?

How could I have righted the ship if I wasn't even told the ship was sinking?

It's akin to professors who don't grade papers before the next one is due. I wasn't told what the problems were, so I had no opportunity to address them. If not for me and my professional development, why hadn't anyone done differently, at least for the benefit of the clients and partners I worked for? My weaknesses came with high stakes not just for my career but for the firm and its legal matters.

Instead of serious critiques in once-a-year performance reviews, someone could have said, "You know, I wasn't satisfied with your work product on that last assignment. Let's sit down and talk about what you could have done differently." If I was so likable, receptive to feedback, and had some strong qualities, as my reviews indicated, why had no one done this?

During the pandemic, I started volunteering at the front desk of the San Francisco SPCA's adoptions center. Recently, a woman asked for a business card with the shelter hours. I explained that her best source for that information was the website.

"That's not going to happen," she said dismissively. "Can you get me a business card?"

I asked her to wait while I checked around. I learned that the SPCA, a non-profit, simply didn't use business cards.

"I'll get you the info," I called back to the woman from the doorway of the office of the adoptions manager, who was neatly writing the shelter hours and phone number on a Post-It for her.

I saw the woman throw up her hands in aggravation. "I just need a phone number!" she yelled.

"That's what I'm getting for you," I called back calmly.

I handed the Post-It to the woman, who was nearly apoplectic for having to wait 120 seconds for the exact information that she'd requested, all of which was easily accessible on the robust website, which she refused to view. "I just needed a phone number!" she repeated and left in a huff.

I thought a lot about the encounter afterwards, trying to figure out what had been so off. True to form, in my quest to slot and characterize and make analogies, I also wondered how the encounter might tie in somehow to the story of my law firm life that was consuming me. I realized that the woman was aggravated because she believed that the shelter *should have* business cards. Her expectations conflicted with what *is*, causing her aggravation. (As a therapist friend likes to say, "Wouldn't you rather live in the real world?")

Was I being just like that woman, *unreasonably* upset that the law firms didn't operate the way I believed they should?

At Thelen, probably yes. I *wish* I'd been in a supportive environment where my skills were boosted or groomed instead of criticized behind my back or once a year in a review. But that's simply the way it was — it wasn't unquestionably wrong. As one lawyer friend who read this manuscript said, "My experience was similar to Scott's description — everybody sank or swam as fast as they could from island to island, switching who they were working with — and even practice areas — hoping not to be eaten by the shark. If they were very lucky, they eventually found someone who would not only give them work, but train them, mentor them and support them as they progressed to senior associates. Those lucky people were the minority and they were mostly men. Things have gotten a little better on this front since the '90's. But even without the assholery that you described, if you started work in 1993 thinking that you would or should be getting mentored and trained, you would have been disappointed."

Looking back, it was unrealistic to expect mentorship or transparency at Thelen. And what happened there is hardly my biggest beef with Big Law. But it's another illustration of structural and systemic problems in law firms. My Thelen experience was merely disappointing. But at Schiffer Mulligan, the rumors and gossip, the exclusion, the meanness — all of which permanently disadvantaged my burgeoning career — was unequivocally, statutorily *wrong*.

***

Thelen labor partner Gil and I became and stayed friends. I worked a lot for him, though I wouldn't go so far as to call him a mentor. To me, a mentor sits you down and walks you through mistakes you made and how you could have approached an assignment or project better. Not one lawyer I ever worked for — at Schiffer Mulligan or at Thelen, not even Gil — ever did that.

When I Zoomed with Gil in 2023 about my work at Thelen, he, like most sources, said his memory of that time wasn't great. But he did remember an oral argument that he assigned to me, and I cringed thinking about it. "I had to jump in to make a point because you weren't understanding the judge's question," he recalled. I, too, remember that embarrassing appearance and feeling so humiliated.

"Malley very quickly formed an opinion that you were not a good attorney," Gil added, referring to the chain-smoking partner. "I didn't agree with that but once Malley formed an opinion of people, that was it."

I dug in, asking Gil about my skills and flaws. "Your writing and research were fine," Gil said. "Trust me, I've had, oh my God, horrible associates. I can think of three other associates with terrible performance. You were not in that category."

I asked what else he remembered of me about that time. "I remember you trying to boost your confidence about yourself. You lacked a belief in yourself that you should have had. I remember thinking, 'C'mon, you've got all this going for you.'"

When I detailed for Gil, today an employment lawyer on the plaintiffs' side, the litany of experiences I had at Schiffer Mulligan, he confirmed that it's the kind of case he would take as a plaintiff's lawyer today. But, he added, he'd give me the same warnings that Mark Rudy and Cliff Palefsky had. "It might have been a career-ender," Gil said. "With the Internet, every employer you applied to after could look up whether you'd sued a former employer. It'd be a blot on your record."

I was fired from Thelen in 1996 after two years of practice there. I was generously given three months to leave. Interestingly, it was Jan Bent, the lawyer who wrote the memo she wanted in my personnel file, who told me she disagreed with the termination decision.

As painful as it was to have the final nail put in the coffin of my legal career, I was strangely relieved. That weekend of my last law firm performance review, I went to dinner with my parents. My mom observed that my shoulders had already dropped two inches.

Thelen was my second and final attempt at practicing law. I'd been out of law school just three years. Looking back, maybe I should have tried a completely different kind of law job, one suited to my sensibilities — maybe something in-house at a non-profit organization or in a government office. But I didn't even try. Two shots at being an associate and I had failed. I was a terrible, unredeemable lawyer. Just 27, I felt as if my worth had been determined by a unanimous group decision: THUMBS DOWN.

On my final day at Thelen, Jim, the co-head of the labor department who'd praised my writing skills, practice development skills and "pleasant personality," hadn't come by my office or even sent an email to say goodbye. In fact, I hadn't heard from him at all in the weeks since I'd been fired. That final afternoon, I asked Gil why that was and Gil surmised that Jim just "felt bad." That a grown man didn't have the courage to say goodbye to the associate he'd worked with for two years who he'd had a hand in firing incensed me. I dialed into his voicemail and left a message that went something like, "I know you know that it's my last day here. I just wanted to say it was nice working with you and I wish you well." I was always taught that just because someone else doesn't show class doesn't mean that you shouldn't. But, admittedly, I also wanted him to feel bad — not for firing me but for avoiding me like a coward afterwards.

***

A few months after my departure from Thelen, a lawyer there and I met for dinner. I learned that soon after I left, this lawyer confessed to department head Linus about feeling badly that Thelen had let me go. But Linus apparently replied dismissively, "Ah, don't worry about it. She was caught having sex in a conference room when she worked at Schiffer Mulligan."

For years I vacillated between finding that hilarious (especially because I didn't have sex *at all* that year, let alone in the office) and deeply disturbing. But years later, when the #metoo movement swept the culture, I emailed Linus.

Jan. 14, 2019

Dear Linus —

Every once in a while, I think about how, after I left Thelen, a partner there confided in me that you had reported that I had been caught having sex in the office of my previous law firm. I have long told myself that confronting you about that absurd lie was not worth the emotional energy better devoted to my family and my career as a legal journalist. But Trump and the #metoo movement have changed that. As a 50-year old woman, I am telling you that not only did I not have sex in any law firm office ever, the nearly funny fact is that I did not even have sex AT ALL the entire year that I worked at that previous law firm. I was a terrible lawyer, an indisputable fact that I own. But you should own the fact that you spread a disgusting, misogynistic rumor about a young female lawyer who did absolutely nothing to you ever. You probably haven't thought about this in decades — that has been your privilege as part of the patriarchy. But I haven't forgotten — and it still hurts.

Jan. 14, 2019

Erin: So sorry that this happened to you! Whoever that partner is, that partner was/is not telling you the truth. The problem with being a successful practitioner is that people attribute awful things to them for their own personal reasons. At Thelen I was in a number of special positions and knew well not to engage in that kind of behavior. I advised the firm on employment issues, counseled others not to engage in harmful behavior, and engaged in sex harassment training to ensure Thelen employees did not engage in illegal or even arguably illegal conduct. I cannot speak for other ex-Thelen partners, but maybe whoever informed you mixed me up with another person. I can assure you, I did not spread rumors about anyone's personal life then or since. Your email below is the first time I have heard anything about your personal life even remotely tied to sex. Regardless, again, I am truly sorry that the conversation with the person responsible ever occurred.

Jan. 14, 2019

Linus — I don't believe you, though I certainly understand why you feel compelled to send such a message. (I wasn't THAT bad of a lawyer.) The partner who told me this has the utmost integrity and wouldn't have lied....I'd even include the person in this conversation to call your bluff but I'm content in having said my piece. You can sort out the rest.

Linus's obnoxious response — to deny wrongdoing by asserting *how important he is* — was patently unsurprising. It was another example of my own lived experience being invalidated by a powerful male lawyer.

My emailing Linus so many years later also shows that I was slowly regaining confidence and power. I still remained locked in the narrative of having been a terrible lawyer, but I was also tapping into the periphery of the abuse in Big Law before diving into its center.

Chapter Seventeen

1997

On my first day on campus in 1997 as a Stanford graduate student, I walked on a path from the parking lot to McClatchy Hall for orientation with the small group of my fellow journalism master's degree students. The McClatchy building was at the head of the legendary "Oval," a large patch of grass at the end of Palm Drive. The Oval is largely responsible for Stanford's reputation as a country club because, on most days, it's populated with undergrads playing volleyball and frisbee and sunning themselves on beach towels. I was starting graduate school in 1997, an El Niño year that saw more rain than California had seen in many years. But on that first day, the weather still had a late summer vibe.

I plodded along that path, wearing a backpack for the first time in six years and wondering what I would soon encounter. Would I be the sole "old lady" of 29 amidst fifth-year seniors getting a master's on top of their undergrad degree? Would my limited success getting first-person essays — on topics like being a newbie lawyer and visiting my sister in Spain — published in legal trade publications like *The Recorder* and free neighborhood rags like *The Noe Valley Voice* translate into any aptitude for "real" journalism?

I shifted the backpack on my shoulders and looked around, taking in the palm trees and the perfectly manicured flora.

"ON YOUR LEFT!" someone shouted at me from behind. Startled and confused, I instinctively stepped...to my left, as if the call was an instruction. I narrowly missed getting hit by a guy on a bike.

"Jesus!" he chided as he barreled past me.

I stood frozen, my heart racing. I wasn't used to cyclists. I lived in San Francisco where I walked on sidewalks and cyclists used the streets. I'd gone to college at UC Berkeley where bikes weren't allowed on campus.

On your left must mean "I'm on your left — move aside," I realized.

I am a fucking idiot.

There's a reason Stanford already rejected me twice — for both college and law school. This master's program clearly made an error admitting me.

I am too stupid to be here.

This is how I talked to myself after my time in Big Law. For *decades.*

I squeezed my eyes shut, willing my heart's pounding to slow and imploring the voice in my head to quiet down. I continued toward the McClatchy building wondering if I was making a huge mistake.

After I left Thelen in 1996, I found a job as a writer at CCH, Inc., a stalwart publisher of legal case books. As part of the interview, I was put in a room and given 30 minutes to read a court opinion about a worker's compensation case and then write a short summary, including the facts, decision and legal reasoning. I walked out of the room and handed the interviewer what I'd written, feeling strangely flushed and exhausted.

The following morning, I was called with an offer for exactly half the pay I'd been making as a lawyer at Thelen. I accepted, relieved to have any income stream at all. I was still in the apartment that Mike and I were supposed to share. In the three years since I'd first moved in, it went from being a financial stretch to being a bit of a deal. San Francisco's Marina District was booming, and because of the city's rent control policies, what I was paying was suddenly on par with or even less than what friends were paying for smaller one-bedrooms and studios. But with the drastic salary reduction, I'd need to cancel cable, nix a gym membership, curb my burrito delivery habit and generally cut costs in every possible way. Many of my friends were finally earning decent incomes after being out of college for six years. But I was in the thick of the lean years.

The day before I was to start at CCH, I received a call from the woman who hired me. The company, based in Chicago, had just announced that morning that it would be closing its California outpost within a year. Did I still want to come work there? she asked.

Yes, I told her.

I have no other options.

When, I wondered, could I get a career off the ground?

I started at CCH the next morning as planned. I wore a cranberry suit and stuck out as the newbie among the few hundred other employees, many also former lawyers, wearing jeans. On my second day, I, too, wore jeans and began what turned out to be a perfect interim job. I had no idea what I'd do once CCH shut down its California office in nine or ten months. All California employees were invited to transfer to CCH's Chicago office, but I knew I'd never do that no matter how much I ended up loving the job.

And I did enjoy my time at CCH. Set high up on a hill above the Northgate Mall in San Rafael in Marin County, CCH's building had a retracting roof that was opened many afternoons, letting in refreshing air and sunlight. In addition to the uber casual dress, which I loved, I had a reverse commute that I think about fondly every time I hear a song from Jewel's Pieces of You album. I listened and sang along to that album on loop during the 25-minute drive.

CCH's protocol required that you work eight hours a day, but the company didn't care when you came in or left. I soon figured out that if I ate lunch at my desk while working, I could leave my apartment in northern San Francisco at 7:30 in the morning, cross the Golden Gate Bridge, be at my desk by 8 a.m., do my work, leave at 4 p.m. and greet Mensch in my apartment by 4:30 p.m. when the sun was still out, hours before my former Big Law colleagues would be stepping foot into their own homes.

The work at CCH was easy and surprisingly interesting. It was there I honed my ability to swiftly read complex information and distill it into its crispest form, skills that I first discovered as an AP History student and served me later as a legal affairs journalist. I also learned a lot about worker's compensation and safety law. One case I read still haunts me — a young woman worked in some kind of factory operating some kind of machine. One day, she bent down to pick up something she'd dropped. Her long hair got caught in the machine and she was scalped to death. The court determined that the employer should have provided proper protective headwear.

I made tons of friends at CCH. Marin County has a reputation for its laid-back, upper class hippie vibe and the CCH crowd was no exception. It was comprised largely of former lawyers with a Marin flair. Corporate's nearly year-long notice of the California office closure did nothing to inspire productivity. I remember many lunchtime picnics at China Camp, a nearby state park, and hilarious afternoon breaks on the second-floor balcony discussing the pros and cons of nut milks (it was 1996, after all) and the latest "Party of Five" episode.

In my first month at CCH, I didn't think too much about what I'd do next. I was focused on catching my breath after three years in law. I knew I wanted to do something with writing. And I knew I didn't want my law degree to go to waste. For a few years, I'd been doing some part-time work at Hastings, teaching legal research and writing and moot court to first-year law students. I considered throwing my hat into the ring at the centralized, national hub for full-time writing professor positions. But I didn't know how qualified — or passionate — I was. I also didn't want to leave San Francisco. I was 28 — it was risky to start laying down roots elsewhere. Also, I was sensing a shift in the tenor of the Hastings classes I was teaching. When I began the adjunct work several years before, the students were hard-working and committed. But the most recent class of first-years were disinterested (blowing off assignments and class) and, worse, entitled (expecting to receive a "P" in the pass-fail class anyway).

It was hard to believe that after three years of law school, passing the bar exam and three years of law practice, I was still wondering how I was going to earn a living.

I remember the precise moment when I came up with a potential plan. I was on a trip with my mom and I was in a hotel bathroom — odd that these are the details I *do* remember — and had one of those light bulb moments.

What if I became a journalist who reports and writes about legal issues?

It was early fall then, the perfect time to apply to journalism programs. I spent the next several months preparing for the GRE, inserting into my computer a floppy disk of a $60 program that would re-teach me math, which I hadn't taken since 1986, my senior year in high school. (My math SAT score was 10 points over the minimum required to exempt me from UC Berkeley's math requirement, which was a godsend because I would have been eaten alive in even a basic math class there.)

I believe I scored in the 60th percentile on the math portion of the GRE. But I aced the verbal and analytical reasoning sections. Gil from Thelen wrote one of my letters of recommendation. (I remember a line to the effect of, "She performed the role of associate to my satisfaction," a way around the fact that I'd been fired from his firm.)

I wrote my application essay in the form of a newspaper article, interviewing my friends and family about me so that it would show my burgeoning reporting skills and enabled me not to have to write directly about my legal career. I was deeply ashamed how my three-year foray into Big Law ended.

I was admitted to the three graduate journalism schools I applied to: Stanford, UC Berkeley and Columbia. Stanford offered me a two-thirds scholarship. I called Columbia, the premiere program in the country, to see if it might match that, but I never received a call back. Berkeley's program was two years and Stanford's was just one. Because I wasn't one hundred percent sure that I wanted to be a journalist, I decided to go for the cheaper, shorter Stanford program. I figured that even if I decided I didn't want to be a journalist, I'd never regret getting a degree from Stanford.

On that first day when I stepped left when a cyclist was "on my left," I was intimidated and, despite my ten months at CCH, still beat up from my three years in law. One of the first things I did at Stanford was seek a therapist through campus health. I was assigned to Trudy, who was one of the best therapists I've ever had. She was non-judgmental and practical, giving me worksheets to complete to begin rebuilding my self-esteem. My sessions with her helped, but I still moved through the world with tremendous self-doubt accompanied by a conviction that my feelings didn't matter. I had a hard time even coming to opinions — I was easily swayed by arguments on both sides, particularly when it came to interpersonal issues. I continued to doubt my worthiness for anything, and it showed in the romantic relationships I pursued. Specifically, I was quite in love then with a close guy friend who knew how I felt but wouldn't take the relationship to the next level. We spent a lot of time together, talking about life and love over beers at "our" bar just off Chestnut Street, and he called me every single night before he went to bed. Yet he wouldn't give a romantic relationship a try. I let myself take scraps — fielding the late-night calls, listening to how his dates went. And I allowed this treatment to go on and on and on.

I spent that rainy year at Stanford looking for Chelsea Clinton, a freshman, on campus (I saw her once), and becoming a Stanford women's volleyball groupie. It was nourishing to be back on a college campus after years in stuffy law firms. I wrote for *The Stanford Daily* and *Stanford Magazine*. I made friends in my program that I still have today, including one of my professors. I earned straight A's and even won the Reader's Digest Excellence in Journalism Award, which came with a monetary gift that covered the final third of tuition for the program. I loved that year at Stanford.

I graduated in May 1998 and a few weeks later started as an intern at *The Daily Journal*, a publication owned by Charlie Munger, who was Warren Buffett's right-hand man. I made minimum wage. A few months later, when a full-time position opened, I was hired as a reporter covering law firms and the business of law. I made slightly more than minimum wage and had the worst benefits in the history of my career. But it was a fascinating time. Big firms were folding in favor of mid-sized and boutique firms (it would be a few years before Thelen finally succumbed), elite law firm partners were being hired away by consulting firms, Silicon Valley lawyers were on the cutting edge of...everything, shifting to casual dress 24/7 and, like their clients, adding foosball tables to the common areas of their low-lying buildings, a sharp contrast to the San Francisco high-rises where Schiffer Mulligan and Thelen were.

At that time, San Francisco was the only city in the country with two competing daily legal newspapers: *The Daily Journal* and *The Recorder*. I had a direct competitor at *The Recorder*, which made the job extra fun as we worked our sources hard to scoop each other. I had an aptitude for cultivating sources, which meant that influential and in-the-know attorneys called me — rather than my competitor at *The Recorder* — with tips and scoops. My success at the job proved that my "interpersonal skills," which Jasper Brook maligned at Schiffer Mulligan, were just fine. I got to know several terrific, powerful female lawyers who made me wonder whether I would have made it in law under their mentorship.

I loved pounding out stories on deadline and seeing my byline above the fold the next morning. I'd always been a strong writer and the job played to my inherent abilities. I loved that once the paper was put to bed, my work for the day was unequivocally done. Longer-term feature stories could be worked on during slower news days, so I never once had to work late nights or on a weekend — and I had zero guilt about that.

I was great at that job — cultivating sources, breaking stories with real significance to the legal community, and writing strong pieces on tight deadlines — and felt that I was finally earning my (meager) keep in a way I never had at Schiffer Mulligan or Thelen. The Daily Journal Corporation was unbelievably stingy but the culture of the San Francisco newsroom was collegial rather than clubby. The editorial structure meant that I got immediate feedback on my story pitches as well as my writing. Mentoring was built into the job framework. If it wasn't for the absurdly awful pay and benefits, I might have stayed in that newsroom for the rest of my career.

That year, I met the man who would become my husband. We met casually first at a barbecue at a mutual friend's house, a friend from my Thelen days. A few weeks later, we spoke by phone when I happened to interview him — then the hiring partner at his law firm — for a *Daily Journal* story I was writing about an increase in associate salaries. He's a wonderful person — reliable, honest, full of integrity — the complete opposite of Mike.

When a venture capital friend (also a former lawyer) told me about a company she was working with that was looking for people, I jumped on the dot-com bandwagon, spending about eight months as the news editor at Productopia, a *Consumer Reports*-like online publication. By this time, I'd been around the block enough to see quite early on that my direct superiors at Productopia — all men — were self-important, uninteresting and (as Michelle Obama famously said) "not that smart." Unsurprisingly, it was one of the very first dot-coms to implode.

That job ended not long before my wedding, so I decided to freelance for a few months, writing for magazines like *San Francisco Attorney Magazine*, the *ABA Journal*, and the now-defunct *California Lawyer Magazine*.

I got married in February 2001. Reggie, Irv, Brian, Gil and several other former Thelen lawyers attended the wedding. Irv even flew across the country to be there. Having them there meant so much to me. It showed that despite all the shitty events of those law firm years, I'd managed to make and keep a handful of wonderful friends. Their presence showed that kind, smart people whom *I* deeply respected wanted to be and stay my friend despite it all.

Less than two months after getting married, I got pregnant and decided to continue freelancing for the foreseeable future.

Fifteen months to the day after my son was born, I gave birth to my daughter. I freelanced for the next nearly 20 years, scheduling calls with lawyers, judges and general counsels around school volunteering and chaperoning field trips. I finished every workday around 2:30 p.m. when I got ready to pick my kids up from school.

I wrote profiles of prominent lawyers and judges. I wrote about business law trends like emerging practice specialties and the influence of Silicon Valley culture on white-shoe law firms. I got paid anywhere from $1/word to, say, $1,000 for a longer piece. I was hired to ghostwrite for lawyers who were asked to write articles for trade magazines but didn't have the time (or, frankly, the skill) to do so. In my extra time, I wrote several women's fiction novels, all in service of my childhood quest to write books like Judy Blume. Most years, I made around $20,000 to $30,000, a fraction of what I'd earn had I stayed in private law practice.

Friends and colleagues comment frequently about my industriousness. I was the primary caregiver for my children, something I took very seriously, only half-jokingly referring to myself as our family's Chief Operating Officer. My byline appeared in law school alumni magazines and other national legal publications, with editors reaching out to me again and again with freelance story assignments. In addition to the women's fiction novels, I also wrote three contemporary romance novels in a single year under a pen name.

I turned helping friends' kids with school application essays into an actual side hustle for money, brainstorming with high school seniors about their college admissions essays and then editing them. I held time-consuming leadership positions — head of the parents association, admissions committee co-chair, annual fundraiser co-chair — at my kids' schools, from preschool all the way through high school. I ran a marathon and two half marathons. (I deeply identify with the meme that reads, "Oh, you're running a marathon? What are you running from? YOUR FEELINGS?") I learned to play Mah Jongg and took Spanish classes. I knit sweaters and socks and hats. So many hats. I got a 200-hour yoga teacher certification and volunteered teaching yoga to public high school students. I became a Court Appointed Special Advocate for a young man in the foster care system.

In other words, for 25 years, I kept very, very busy. It was an obsession with productivity and a trauma response. Upon reflection, it's clear I kept myself busy to avoid the humiliation of being given no work at Schiffer Mulligan. I needed to feel that I was earning my keep, particularly because society so values productivity. My negative ego, the one telling me I was worthless, not good enough, not doing enough, drove almost all of it. Like all humans, I desperately needed to feel valued. As June Carter Cash said, I was just "trying to matter."

All of these projects also kept me on a path of forward momentum, enabling me to avoid sitting still and being with my self-loathing and pain. I didn't want to face myself, my past, the shame I felt in the choices and mistakes I'd made and the "weak" way I'd behaved, leading to ouster at not one but two prestigious law firms.

Despite the Stanford degree and the hundreds of bylined articles and the knitting and running and yoga and volunteering, I struggled — and still struggle — with feeling that I'm not good at anything. My 22-year-old son, an alto sax player, was better at riffing on stage at 16 than I am at *anything*. At least that's what my inner voice says. To quote from the epic monologue in the "Barbie" film, "We always have to be extraordinary, but somehow we're always doing it wrong."

At bookstore events and on podcasts promoting my novels, I was often asked about my transition from lawyer to writer, and frequently I'd be told that I was "brave" to have left the law. That made me squirm, almost nauseous. I'd deflect, but not go so far as to confess that I'd been, essentially, kicked out of the profession. I felt the opposite of brave — too ashamed to reveal what had really happened. Only now, after Kelli's own revelation had me re-thinking the cause-and-effect nature of my failure in law, can I more openly discuss the details. Maybe I hadn't been a terrible lawyer. Maybe I hadn't been immature, weak, pathetic.

Eleanor Roosevelt famously said that no one can make you feel inferior without your consent. Eleanor was great, but this is distinct *bullshit*. When someone (or a group of someones) chips away at your self-esteem, it's hard to have the...self-esteem to withstand that. Roosevelt's statement was designed to foster a sense of self-worth, of one's own agency. But she had the rare privilege of operating at the highest echelons of society, of having the willing ear of the most powerful leader on earth. Her statement doesn't apply to individuals who are subject to institutions with power differentials, whether explicit or de facto. In Big Law, powerful men and women wielded their positions in ways that, deliberate or not, made me feel inferior, even worthless. I believed what I was supposed to believe — that I'd made a terrible mistake in trying to be a Big Law lawyer, maybe even a lawyer at all. I was not analytical or tough or even competent.

Of course, I've been in therapy for years. But until recently, I was ashamed to admit to anyone, even to therapists, that I'd been fired. It's a measure of how much shame I felt that my husband of more than 22 years didn't even know until he read a draft of this book. Sharing with my husband what really happened during my three years in Big Law gave him a new understanding of me, his partner of more than two decades. My weird nightmares, my struggles with self-esteem...it finally made sense to him. Interestingly, too, he grew more compassionate towards women associates in his own firm, including one with a less-than-positive performance review. He re-evaluated how he could help her gain the skills she was lacking rather than just informing her that they were lacking.

Before, I held my past close, slotting it into a tiny compartment in my brain in an effort to regain control over my reputation. Outwardly, I chalked up abandoning my legal career, my original life plan, to the profession simply being a wrong fit for my constitution. That may ultimately have been true, but I never got a real chance to figure it out on my own terms. I didn't grasp until recently that the way I was treated was a form of gender abuse, a traumatic experience that I still feel the effects of. I didn't understand — until my conversation with Kelli — that talking about the experience, that shining a light on it, might dislodge the pain and let it finally move through and out of me.

Seeing my therapist's compassionate expression once I finally shared what had happened showed me that, like Kelli's situation, there was a wholly different way I could look at those years and myself. After 19 years of sessions with her, I believe she finally understood why I had so little self-confidence despite outward accomplishments. I'm slowly and belatedly learning that my value is not something to be measured in accomplishments or salary. In fact, it's not to be measured at all. My value — like everyone's — is not something to prove or earn. It's intrinsic. It's a birthright.

Sharing the story with my kids was also cathartic. My husband is a wildly respected real estate lawyer, landing on every "best of" list there is. My kids have grown up observing him at the top of his game (albeit also constantly overworked, under-rested, lamenting selling his time in 15-minute increments, and being at the mercy of pushy clients). I didn't want my kids to know how badly I'd crashed and burned in the exact same profession. But when I told them — at ages 20 and 21 — what had happened at Schiffer Mulligan, they, too, listened with compassion.

"Mom," my daughter responded, "you always joke that you were a rotten lawyer. But you were never even given a proper chance!"

With Kelli's inspiration and through the process of working on this story, I'm trying to give myself the grace that I would insist that others give themselves.

I'm not a high-powered lawyer but I'm...inquisitive, with a relentless drive to get to the heart of issues. I hardly make any money but...I'm a thoughtful friend. I don't manage a team of professionals, but...I'm practical and efficient.

"The one thing I know without question that I'm good at is being a mom," I told my therapist when we were talking about this recently. My children are terrific young adults. I credit them, not myself, for their talents and ambitions. But I do believe that my parenting contributed at least in part to their being kind, engaged, interested, polite, genuine, honest, compassionate, self-aware young adults with strong familial and friend relationships as well as success in their chosen fields. Based on my own lack of preparation for what happened at Schiffer, my parenting also included deliberately refraining from "fixing" their problems, as tempting as it was sometimes.

I drilled feminist principles — gender equality, the power (often stifled) of women, etc. — into both my son and daughter. It would never occur to my son to treat a woman the way Mike, Ben, Jasper Brook or Dixon Long treated me. My daughter, all 5"2' of her, knows how to set boundaries and appreciates and conveys her worth.

My therapist then reminded me of another First Lady's famous pronouncement. "If you bungle raising your children," Jackie Kennedy once said, "I don't think whatever else you do matters very much."

When, in high school, my son was asked to describe his parents, he wrote, "Loving, responsible." It was one of the greatest compliments of my life.

As for my beloved cat Mensch, he lived for 19 years, during my own most formative years: I adopted him when I was 24 and he died when I was 43. He'd been at my side through the end of law school, my painful years as a lawyer, different boyfriends and jobs and apartments and graduate school, purring next to me as I became a wife and a mother. I'm proud that I gave him, my first pet, a safe and loving home for all those years. I've since had two fabulous dogs, but there was no soul-deep connection like I'd had with Mensch. To this day, a purring cat is my favorite sound in the world.

Chapter Eighteen

2023

That year at Schiffer Mulligan cost me in many ways.

I lost 17 pounds due to stress.

I spent money on a workplace harassment attorney, on therapy, on an apartment meant for two.

I lost the ability to be a friend to myself. As I slowly revealed details of the year to my therapist in 2023, she described it as "self-esteem murder." I wrote a whole novel, which remains unpublished, about an extremely capable woman who couldn't trust her own judgment about anything. I have friends who not only trust but easily promote their own feelings and opinions. I secretly study them.

My friend's young adult daughter's nickname is "Hurricane Peri" because she has a big personality and a distinct spark for life. She's the kind of girl who finds herself on the Jumbotron at a football game. But when I saw Peri recently, her affect was flat, and she seemed so unhappy. It was upsetting to observe. An auditor at a big accounting firm, Peri was working 80-hour weeks for a client she hated. I realized that she is just about the age that I was when I started my Schiffer Mulligan journey — the prime of our lives — and that my own drastic loss of light must have mirrored hers. It made me so sad.

My own 25th year caused me to lose faith in myself. Every gain I'd made — from graduating college with honors to being selected for law review to the praising memo from Jon Streeter at Orrick — was entirely disregarded in my own mind. Later, after the Stanford degree and awards, after editors sent me freelance assignment after assignment while complimenting me on my writing, my mind simply refused to internalize those gains, refused to let them buoy and fuel me.

A few months ago, a friend invited me to join a casual pickleball game. At that point, I considered myself a low-intermediate player. I'd taken classes and played in drop-in games. I wasn't a star but could hold my own on the court. That evening, however, I tanked. For some inexplicable reason, the majority of my hits went straight into the net. Not only did that embarrass me in front of my friends but, worse, it stopped the momentum of the game for everyone. The fun of pickleball is the back-and-forth. When the ball hits the net, all that fun stops. The more my hits went into the net, the more I got into my head and then the worse it got. I have nice friends so none of them complained or even commented on my playing, but I had to hold back tears.

In my car afterwards, I sat frozen, unable to move in a cloud of inexplicable shame, completely out of proportion to what had occurred. But it brought up familiar emotions of embarrassment, of feeling I'm not earning my keep, of not being worthy. It was all a throwback to my time in Big Law.

Of course, when it comes to the real monetary cost of my year at Schiffer Mulligan, I lost vast income potential. Many senior law firm partners in San Francisco — which I would be had I stayed in law — make upwards of $1 million a year. During my most profitable year working part-time as a freelance legal affairs journalist, I earned about $60,000.

A simple Google search reveals that Ben is worth at least $11 million.

According to LinkedIn, Mike has had no fewer than 11 jobs since 1994, many at the CEO level. Today, he runs a company that a large online retailer purchased for nearly $300 million.

But while they outpaced me financially, maybe these men were broken too. Maybe grinding away in Big Law for decades resulted in an emotional emptiness, a kind of emptiness that would cause them to treat a young female colleague the way they did. Men who could do many of the shameful things they did must have been insecure and in a dark place. I'm working to see nuance in complicated situations. Maybe there's room for compassion at the deep sadness inherent in Big Law life.

Chapter Nineteen

2023

Though we're Jewish, my children spent their kindergarten through eighth grade years at a Friends School. There, they — and I — learned the Quaker concept of "seasoning." Quakerism's emphasis on deferring important actions in favor of thoughtful reflection speaks to me because it supports processing and invites questions, latent unease, and true feelings rise to the surface of the mind. Clarity, Quakers realize, comes over time and in small amounts.

The events at Schiffer Mulligan in 1993 and 1994 changed the course of my life. Re-evaluating those events in my 50's helped me understand not only what happened but who I am. I am finally moving *into* grief and trauma from 30 years ago instead of away from it.

In reporting my story, I pondered certain what-if questions:

Did the secretary who gave me the Brook memo help me or do me a disservice? What might've happened had I never seen it?

What if Ben hadn't handed my parents his business card at a party?

What if I'd sued Schiffer Mulligan, taken a settlement, took some time off and skipped the unfulfilling years at Thelen, going instead straight into legal journalism?

I struggled to find meaning in what had happened. Eventually, after many months, I stopped trying to force it. And perhaps that was the lesson. At 55, I'm no longer exerting so much energy in striving. Now, when it comes to personal goals or acceptance in social communities, I pause to ask myself, "*Why* do I want in on this?" I'm abiding by the concept of "volunteers not recruits" when it comes to relationships. I now notice when I'm unnecessarily clinging, grasping or forcing; I'm learning to simply *allow*. To quote the "Barbie" film again, "I'm just so tired of watching myself and every single woman tie herself into knots so that people like us."

***

I wound down reporting for this story after interviewing every former Schiffer Mulligan colleague that I reached out to — that is, colleagues with knowledge of me, The Club and the events — with a few exceptions.

For example, my dear friend Brian, who was in the summer and first-year class with me, would have been a wonderful contributor to this story. When many Schiffer Mulligan attorneys distanced themselves from me, Brian always supported me. He was one of the two friends who attended my wee last-day lunch at the firm, and he remains my friend to this day. Brian has had many successes in his career — even serving, for a time, as an on-air commentator for MSNBC — and is the loving father of three children. He is also living with ALS and no longer able to speak, which made getting his recollections of this time impossible.

Not surprisingly, I never received responses to emails and postal letters I sent to Jasper Brook or Dixon Long. I can only hope that's because they now know that their callus, misogynistic actions were indefensible. Looking back, I am particularly shocked that those two men were *employment* lawyers. One cannot help but wonder what damage, if any, their judgment caused to individuals and clients?

Despite several attempts, I also did not hear back from Ben Bucknell or David Powell, who still practice law together at a tech company. (In the Fall 2021 Schiffer Mulligan alumni newsletter, Powell was featured. Part of the article read, "David is lucky to have a vacation house in Tahoe and has enjoyed working from home in the mountains, which has allowed him to relax during these stressful times. He would schedule meetings for the afternoon, then go ski for an hour and a half, and then come back to his meetings. He also collects fine wine and considers himself a gourmand.")

The reasons for Ben's, Powell's and Tim Reids's failures to respond to my messages — or Frederick Duncan's choice to stop communicating after I sent him a PDF of my 1994 letter upon my firm departure — are up to the reader's interpretation.

I did not contact management or administrators at Schiffer Mulligan. Not one of the lawyers mentioned in this story works there today. And given that the firm mindlessly sent a "We've Missed You — Join Our Alumni Network" solicitation to a lawyer who nearly sued the firm for hostile work environment sexual harassment, I'm certain that no response of value would have resulted. As for Thelen, it dissolved in 2008.

Throughout the reporting and drafting process, I debated about contacting Mike, to whom I haven't spoken since 1994. On the "pro" side, I was committed to applying the journalistic principles I learned at Stanford and practiced in my career as a legal affairs journalist. Those principles dictated that every "character" in this story has an opportunity to speak on the events. On the "con" side, Mike's capacity for gratuitous cruelty as well as deception is well-documented here. Also, our circles— and, perhaps more importantly, our kids' circles — of association were alarmingly close. I was concerned for my emotional safety as well as my kids'. In the end, with my kids' permission, I landed on the side of preserving my journalistic integrity. As my manuscript neared completion, I sent a brief email to Mike using the address I found on the State Bar website. I wrote, "I'm writing a book about my first year as a lawyer, relying not just on my memories but also on recent interviews with more than a dozen Schiffer Mulligan colleagues as well as memos and emails I've preserved from that year. If you're willing to be interviewed, please let me know and I'll set up a Zoom. Thanks. Erin"

I did not receive a reply. Mike was the one exception to the rule that I gave every potential source two chances to respond. I contacted him once and accepted his silence, fearing that otherwise I'd be "poking the bear."

Before that, Mike had crossed my mind only fleetingly over the years, though I predict The Club will use this book as evidence that I *still* haven't gotten over him. We share a few connections on Facebook and LinkedIn, social constructs that didn't exist back in the early '90's. His profile photos show he has the same overly wide smile and, like most middle-aged men, a lot less hair. Years ago, I saw his name a few below mine on a parent list for kids going to sleepaway camp in Yosemite. Our oldest kids, I noted, were boys the same age but, thankfully, they didn't end up in the same bunk. I did spot him from afar at camp drop-off but I focused on my own family. I doubt he looked at the parent list or noticed me that day.

Several years later, I spotted name tags with his and his daughter's names as I was checking parents into the spring welcome day at the high school my son attended. Those two name tags weren't claimed that day, and a few months later, when the new school year started, I noticed while looking through the student directory that Mike's daughter hadn't ended up enrolling after all. According to sources I interviewed, he's now divorced.

The young woman who started at Schiffer Mulligan in 1993 feels like another person altogether, which, I imagine, is how many 55-year-olds view their 25-year-old selves. I wish I'd been tougher, stronger, more vocal, even if I remained powerless. And I wonder, too, if Mike has changed, if he looks back at himself at that age and wishes he, too, had behaved differently.

I doubt it, though. Several years ago, a friend was looking to buy a house and wanted a referral to a real estate broker. After I found my broker's website, I noticed that none other than Mike was listed as a testimonial. I emailed the broker, with whom I'd become friendly after years of searching for a new house under her guidance.

"I just noticed on your website," I wrote, "that you represented Mike Davenbaum. I dated him many, many years ago."

Within minutes the broker wrote back: "Mike is richer than your husband. But," she added, "your husband is much nicer."

I later understood that while Mike was, in my experience, immature and mean, it was the adults in the room — Ben, most notably — who should have put a stop to what Mike was doing and what other members of The Club, like gossip-y David Powell, enabled. Ben's and others' bystander status, to me, amounts to culpability. I suspect that Ben and the others I never heard from want questionable actions of the past to stay there. After all, while many sources I interviewed began by noting that "it was so long ago," *not one single person* said, "None of that happened."

I brooded about how those important sources who never responded to my interview requests would react to my story. I'm certain that in my pain I did embarrassing things of which I have no recollection, that I'd cringe to be reminded of. But as the author E. Lockhart wrote, "I would rather speak my truth and be laughed at or ignored than stick to what is easy and familiar." I might have behaved immaturely, but anything I did stemmed from sheer *desperation* for someone to be outraged on my behalf.

I also feared being sued for libel, and spent more money than I'm likely to earn this entire year on a media lawyer. This is infuriating because, looking back, *I* could have sued The Club for slander given how profoundly their cruel, casual conversations impacted my career. Exhibit A: Linus, a partner at my *next* firm, hearing and re-telling a disgusting, completely false rumor about me having sex in a Schiffer Mulligan conference room.

***

As I've moved squarely into middle age, I've discovered that names from the deep past sometimes pop into my brain unexpectedly. A year or so ago, the name Lisa Tamblin appeared. Lisa was a girl from elementary school — a little nebbishy and nerdy, with a bit of a lisp. With shame, I recalled memories of teasing and crank calling her with other girls, something she absolutely didn't deserve. I understand now that I participated primarily because as long as there was someone lower on the social totem pole, the other girls wouldn't turn on *me*. As an adult thinking back to that time, I felt sick to my stomach. And then I did what any person would do in 2023: I Googled Lisa. I figured I'd find her on Facebook or LinkedIn and, as I typed in her name, I grew determined to send her a message apologizing for my role in that unkind behavior back in the early 1970's. It took a bit of digging but then I located something.

Her obituary.

Lisa had passed away in her early 40's from breast cancer. Learning this, I felt even more sick and for days I was saddened in a way I couldn't explain.

Had my name ever popped into the heads of Ben or Powell or Brook or Long the way Lisa's did for me? Given that some of the people I interviewed, like Elizabeth, confessed to not even remembering me at all, it's doubtful. But I'm easy to find online and, unlike Lisa, am still alive. So, if any of them *had* thought of me with remorse, why hadn't they contacted me? That no one reached out — then or years later as #metoo gained momentum — to express remorse about their role in my trauma is nearly as painful as the trauma itself.

While my therapist insisted that Lisa had needed to heal on her own, that my contacting her when she was alive wouldn't have changed much, *I* would so have appreciated a sincere, out-of-the-blue apology from anyone at Schiffer Mulligan. In *Truth and Repair: How Trauma Survivors Envision Justice*, Judith L. Herman refers to the power of acknowledgment, apology and amends. Even a belated *acknowledgement* of the wrongs at Schiffer Mulligan would have gone a long way towards my healing. The muted sorries I received from sources like Frederick and Max weren't enough.

In *The Power of Regret*, Daniel Pink discovered that regret typically falls into four categories, including "lapses in moral judgment." Despite the cultural awakening resulting from #metoo, is it even reasonable to expect lawyers from 1993-1994 Schiffer Mulligan to take stock of how they treated a young female lawyer? How could *I* be the Lisa Tamblin of someone else's life if, as became clear during a couple of my 2023 interviews, they didn't remember me at all? And, yet, which way does that cut: that a young female lawyer who cried in the managing partner's office was *completely unmemorable*?

***

I spent many hours contemplating the difference between actions that were the result of forgivable mistakes and those that represented deep character flaws. I looked up the oath that attorneys must take when admitted to the California Bar. It requires them to promise to conduct themselves "at all times with dignity, courtesy and integrity." If you extend these ethical standards to interpersonal relationships within a law office, this oath was undoubtedly violated. And the nastiness continues today. During several interviews, Schiffer Mulligan alums shit-talked their former colleagues.

I will never know what stories they're telling themselves about that time. And, as I've learned, I cannot force finding an answer.

In my reporting, I was surprised to discover that most everyone was suffering in the law firm environment in one way or another. Elizabeth and Frederick were both powerful partners and yet they had their own ugly exits from the firm. I learned of others' unseen alcoholism, marital problems, State Bar suspensions, and wondered how all that fit into what I experienced.

After more Quaker "seasoning," I concluded that while we have no idea what others are going through, it's not up to the *victims* of abuse or harassment to make allowances. Rather, it's up to the offenders to find appropriate coping mechanisms, to not let their own lives so brutally impact others'. Yes, everybody is going through "something." But it's human decency to ensure that our something doesn't go on to cause somebody else's something. And shouldn't experiencing hardships make us *more* compassionate towards others? Let's all work on healing our wounds instead of spreading the pain.

A lesson *I* took from all of this: *be mindful of your impact.*

***

Recently, I attended a dinner for the partners and spouses of my husband's law firm to celebrate newly elected partners into the firm. Per tradition, one or two partners in the new partner's practice group stood and lauded the new partner to the entire partnership and their spouses, telling funny and earnest stories about the person's excellence at what they do. I've gone to this dinner for many years. This year, though, I held back tears. The new partners were much, much younger than me, and it struck me that, at 55, I would *never* be in a professional situation like this, never be publicly lauded that way. Sitting with this unrealized potential caused real grief.

Recent "lookback" laws in states like New York and California have extended the statute of limitations for childhood sexual abuse claims in recognition of the fact that children may not understand they've been abused until years or decades later. They can be too young, too manipulated or too traumatized to understand that certain behaviors were wrong. (As for Kelli, she did not file suit but settled privately with the high school. To date, the school still has not publicly conducted an investigation into other abuse by the teacher, even though that's all that Kelli wanted from the institution.)

In California, the statute of limitations for filing a hostile work environment claim is one year. I worked for Schiffer Mulligan from 1993 to 1994. If lookback laws applied to sexual harassment claims, I might have filed a suit all these years later.

Fortunately, there is no statute of limitations on exercising a First Amendment right, on freedom of speech. Even if I wouldn't trade my family or anything else that resulted from my departure from Big Law, I want to tell my story. Truth is a complete defense to defamation, and I've provided firsthand evidence, including documents and eyewitness accounts of what happened.

Firm leaders and members of The Club might argue that since many people in power fail to remember me, I've clearly overblown that whole year in my mind. But has any man ever questioned a system that worked well for him but not for others?

Most white men don't know what it's like not to be heard or believed.

Most white men don't know the pain of being excluded.

I was so insignificant as to not be remembered — but it's time to fight systems and institutions that are *set up* to chew up and spit out people deemed to be insignificant. *No one* is insignificant.

***

"What do you want?" That exasperated question — from my employment attorney Mark Rudy's associate when I was deliberating whether to sue Schiffer Mulligan after the Jasper Brook memo — swirled in my brain as I wrote this book.

*What do I want...*now?

One plausible answer is revenge. And of course, that's very, very tempting. But it's also unrealistic. After all, Brook, Long, Mike, Ben, Frederick...they've made their millions, had their glory. And, of course, money isn't a measure of anything, really. I'm also not foolish enough to believe my story will negatively impact these men.

What I do want: *a true moral reckoning for these people.*

I want Jasper Brook and Frederick Duncan and Dixon Long and The Club to own up in their own minds to their actions, to understand that I was not only mistreated but also gaslit.

I want the lawyers at Thelen — especially Malley, who badmouthed me, and Garter, who hired me but wouldn't say goodbye to me, and Linus, who shared a false and malicious rumor about me — to know what really happened at Schiffer Mulligan, not some untruths about me having sex in a conference room. I want all the lawyers I ever worked with to understand that maybe with just a little bit of kind mentoring, I might have overcome that awful first year to grow into a decent lawyer. I want my Thelen friends and contemporaries, who surely heard or suspected that I'd been fired, to know my Big Law origin story.

Most of all, I want others, especially women, to do what Monica Lewinsky, Kelli and now I have done: re-examine our narratives, the stories we tell ourselves about ourselves, and reclaim them. Cognitive scientists have long understood the negativity bias, that tendency to dwell on the negative. In women, I believe, that extends to our own self-images.

I spent decades either emotionally beating myself up or tucking painful memories away in shame. But in pulling apart all the events leading up to my first day at Schiffer Mulligan, I realize that my daughter is right: I simply *never stood a chance.* I'm learning to look at my 24-year-old self — and my current self — with compassion instead of embarrassment or derision.

It's okay to change our minds, to mature and evolve. Some things can only be understood in hindsight, like sitting in one of the backward-facing seats on a train, seeing what you've passed only *after* you've passed it. That's how we know that repeated football collisions cause brain damage. In the 1970's, I was taught that Columbus "discovered" America. Some of my early personal essays were culturally insensitive. I learned. Let's shine daylight onto painful parts of our pasts and integrate them into our lives instead of locking them away in that mental box, where they're sure to fester, infecting other parts of ourselves. Let's honestly re-examine the stories we tell ourselves — or the stories we let others tell us. Let's take ownership of our truth.

Despite her "embarrassing" journals from the 1980's, Kelli was abused by a predator three times her age. Monica Lewinsky had consensual sex with President Clinton but was also unequivocally a victim of gender violence from our culture. I may or may not have been a bad lawyer, but I was in a hostile work environment and experienced institutional gaslighting that altered the course of my entire life.

I'm only now beginning to see what a badass I was to pass the bar, to go to work every day while wondering what firm event I'd be excluded from, what negative untruth was being whispered about me, whether another public photo of me would be defaced. Re-reading the letter I wrote to Frederick upon my 1994 departure, the one that apparently caused him to stop communicating with me in 2023, I see how strong I really was. And when friends who supported this project, including Kelli, comment on how much bravery it takes to tell this story, to confront people who wronged me, I'm resisting the urge to dismiss their praise.

I'm finally, finally beginning to trust myself.

What do I want?

I want this story of love and heartbreak, of gender and sex, of bullying and law to inspire others, especially women, to critically investigate shameful experiences and scrutinize negative self-talk.

Stories are powerful. Reclaim your narrative.

In 2017, I started going by the name Erin. (Background here: https://bit.ly/EGNameChange.) For simplicity and clarity, I changed all references to my old name, which I went by during the years depicted in this book, to Erin.

Dear Reader,

There's a shampoo commercial from the '70's that illustrates the exponential power of word of mouth. A peppy blond declares, "I told two friends about Faberge shampoo. And they told two friends and they told two friends...and so on!" It was a great way to sell hair products 50 years ago, but given the competitive realities of today's publishing industry, word-of-mouth is the *only* way books find an audience.

Although truth is a defense to defamation (and The File proves what happened), some of the players in this story — all experienced litigators — could still sue me as punishment for publishing this book, forcing me to defend what they know is a baseless lawsuit. To protect myself, I hired a libel lawyer for pre-publication review of the manuscript and I purchased libel insurance. These protections cost much more than I'm likely to earn from sales of this book and, to me, this is another example of how that one year at Schiffer Mulligan continues to impact my professional life and income.

Which brings me back to the Faberge commercial. If this story resonated with you, *your personal recommendation or positive review can directly impact its success*. My experience with harassment and workplace bullying took place in California law offices, but versions of it have played out in nearly every industry around the world. So please share *Look What You Made Me Do* with anyone who might benefit from this story of heartbreak and harassment, of triumph over misplaced shame. Thank you for helping this story find its audience.

Warmly,

Erin Gordon

Erin@ErinGordonAuthor.com

Profound thanks to my wise and honest beta readers, several of whom reviewed this manuscript more than once: Emmy, Craig, Kelli, Kerryn, Jill, Tali, Kristin, Leslie, Bruce, Jodi, Lori, Susanne, Robin, Donna, Robert, Willow, Karen E., Megan, Karen Z. and Rachel.

Thank you to the experts, former colleagues and friends who agreed to be interviewed for this book.

Thank you to my lawyer, Charles Glasser, for the expert pre-publication review of *Look What You Made Me Do.*

Thank you to my parents and sister — every day I think about your generosity in putting me through law school. I hope you feel, as I do, that it was worth it despite what happened at "Schiffer Mulligan" and Thelen.

A special thank you to the friends who stuck by me at Schiffer Mulligan when it was unpopular to do so, especially Brian, "Reggie" and "Irv."

To any readers who've experienced harassment, gaslighting (including institutional gaslighting), workplace bullying and related harms — especially long ago when we weren't able to find or support each other via hashtags and social media — I hope it helps you to know that you were not and are not alone.

Erin Gordon is a legal affairs journalist and the author of several novels. She lives in San Francisco. Learn more at ErinGordonAuthor.com.

Read the Opening Chapters of
Erin Gordon's Most Recent Novel
PEEPS

CHAPTER ONE

I had so many questions.

Why had she never tried to understand me? Why had she been so cold to us?

If the situation were reversed and the funeral was for me, *would my mother have attended?*

Just as these thoughts arose, the service ended. The twenty or so guests began to mingle and nibble on bagels and fruit in the restaurant's small private room, my mother's ashes in a modest urn at the head of the table. I excused myself for the restroom, my brain swirling with everything I wish I'd asked before cancer claimed her lucidity.

Through the bathroom's partially cracked window, the squawks of seagulls and the pot my brother was smoking wafted inside. It hit me then.

I was no longer someone's daughter.

At fifty-one, I was an orphan, my father having died suddenly when I was a toddler. I sat on the closed toilet lid, my bones aching as if I'd been hit by a semi. Yet also emerging were the first sparks of what I always imagined I'd feel when my mother was gone: relief.

I washed my hands in the sink just to keep me alone with my thoughts a few moments longer.

I wished I'd asked my mother the seven questions I posed to all my podcast guests. Since she was now dead, what object, I wondered, would she have taken with her to the afterlife? I honestly had no guesses. I'd never been able to grasp what was important to my mother. I just knew it wasn't us.

Alex, my son, would probably take his collection of Stevie Wonder albums on vinyl. My ex-husband Jeff recently volunteered his answer: "I'd bring my wedding ring from my marriage to you," he said, "and the receipt from my first date with Milt — the two loves of my life."

Then another truth struck me as sharply as the almond-scented soap.

I was no longer someone's partner.

I needed to get back to the gathering as the mourners would soon disperse. My brother was still outside smoking so it was up to me to thank everyone who'd paid their respects.

I joined the tiny cluster of my friends who'd come not to say goodbye to my mother but to support me. One handed me a mug of coffee. Another draped her arm around my shoulder. I'd known most of these women for upwards of fifteen years, since our kids were in preschool. We'd seen each other through potty training and tantrums. We'd collaborated about when to allow our kids cell phones and social media access. We'd shared photos of our teens with their learner's permits. Now those kids were college freshmen scattered throughout the country.

Reality smacked me again.

I was no longer an active parent.

"Meg?"

I turned to see Jeff, my ex-husband, arms outstretched. "Milt's gone out to get our car," he said, enveloping me in a hug. He felt, he smelled as he always did, as familiar to me as my own body. "I'll call tomorrow, okay?"

I nodded. "Thank you both."

Soon after, the rest of the guests drifted out with condolences and embraces. Then it was just me and my younger brother Leith. I was settling up with the restaurant when Leith approached me carrying the urn.

"I assume you don't want this?" he said, holding it up like a trophy.

"Uh, that's a hard no," I said. Even if my mother had been warm and loving, the kind of mother I worked so very hard to be, I would have declined.

"I figured. I'll take it." He pulled keys from his pocket and jangled them. "Got a long drive back up north. I'm gonna hit the road. Thanks, Meggie, for, you know, handling everything. Especially these last few weeks."

Our mother died swiftly after a pancreatic cancer diagnosis. I'd arranged her care.

"It's what I do," I said with a shrug.

"Well," Leith said, half hugging me with the arm that wasn't holding our mother's ashes, "now you're free."

It was thrilling and terrifying.

Without parents, a spouse, my son nearby... *Who was I?*

***

Brad and I met up in the shade of a huge Monterey cypress tree outside his house on Adelaide Drive about a mile and a half from my own in Santa Monica. He greeted me with a hug and a sympathetic smile with an extended lower lip that I'd seen from others that morning at the funeral. We walked three blocks to the beachfront path and then sauntered north. It was late afternoon. The sun was bright but turning a warmer shade of orange and the breeze was picking up.

Brad and I had been set up a few weeks before by mutual friends. Attentive and interesting, he was also surprisingly fit and attractive for a fifty-eight-year-old divorcee with three kids. I hadn't dated in twenty-five years but so far he'd made it far less awkward than it could have been. On our first date, we met at a wine bar and talked about books, raising kids and mid-life divorce. The next week we went to a movie that neither of us could concentrate on because the famous actor who was headlining that very film was sitting two rows in front of us. A week ago — two days before my mother died — we grabbed vegan hot dogs at Yum Dog and ate them while watching the sun set over the Pacific

before going to an artist talk at a nearby gallery that his friend owned. We finally kissed that night, a very, very good kiss, the kind you turn over and over in your head, memorizing its breadth and depth so you can conjure it again at will.

"How was the memorial?" Brad asked as we dodged rollerbladers and cyclists. He'd offered to accompany me to the service but I'd declined, explaining that it would be a small gathering — Jeff and Milt, a few of my mother's former co-workers, a handful of my friends. My own son, I explained, wouldn't even be flying home from college to attend. After just three dates, it was far too early for Brad to meet my friends, my ex-husband. It was too early, too, for him to witness first-hand how conflicted, maybe even ambivalent, I was about her death.

"It was nice," I said. "My younger brother spoke. I read some words from my mother's brother Oscar, her only living sibling, who's too old to travel across country. The whole thing lasted less than an hour. I'm just glad it's over." I regretted that last part, fearing I'd over shared or, worse, revealed a callousness he wouldn't like. "Anyway, I'd love to talk about something else. Is that okay?"

"Of course," he said, putting his arm around me the way he did the night we roamed through the art gallery. Jeff had loved me — still loved me — deeply, but he'd never been affectionate like Brad. "Here's something: tell me about Peeps. Since we first met, I've listened to two episodes. And now I have questions."

"Fire away," I said, grateful for the topic shift.

"How'd it start?"

"Short or long answer?"

He looked down and sideways at me and smiled. "Long."

"Okay, so, when I was in college at UCLA, about a hundred years ago, I wrote this column, kind of a man-on-the-street feature, for the Daily Bruin. I was a journalism major and wanted to hone my writing skills. But it turned out I learned way more about the human condition than I did about journalism."

"Go on."

"There's a proverb that goes something like, 'God must have really liked stories because he made so many people.' In stopping random students and faculty on the quad, in asking pointed questions, I discovered that everyone had a story. I could literally never miss, no matter who I interviewed."

"Did you write for newspapers after college?"

I shook my head. "Baby reporters usually have to cut their teeth at small-town papers in Arkansas or North Dakota or other places far, far from LA. I mean, I've only ever lived here."

"Really? Only LA?"

"Yeah. So I knew that, constitutionally, I'm just not cut out for that kind of uncertainty or isolation."

"You sell yourself short."

"Also, Jeff and I were seriously dating then and he was staying in LA after graduation. So I took a PR job downtown. For a think tank devoted to water resources. I churned out press releases about transfer water rights and wetlands permitting. You know, fascinating stuff. I worked there for a few years until I had Alex. Then I stayed home."

"My ex also stayed home with our kids. She referred to herself as the family's COO."

"I like that."

We reached a beachfront shack on the path. Wordlessly, as if we were in sync, we got in line. The scent of coconut tanning lotion on the teenaged girls behind us commingled with the fishy seaside wind. We ordered two decaf iced mochas, and returned to the path, heading south, back the direction we came. Nearby herons clucked their familiar *go-go-go* landing call.

"Then what?" Brad said, shaking his cup, the ice sounding like dice. "Then what what?"

"How'd you go from staying home with your son to starting a podcast?"

"Ah, right," I said, mock smacking my head. "When Alex started high school four years ago and needed me less, my friend Dana hired me to write for her legal newsletter. It was nice to have a paycheck again. But the work was — still is — boring. I thought back to how much I'd loved

writing that column in college, how I loved making art out of *life*." "Did you apply for newspaper jobs? You know, like pitching that same

kind of column?"

Sipping my mocha, I shook my head. "Who'd hire a forty-something part-time legal newsletter writer? A woman who'd done a bit of PR ten, fifteen years ago? A writer whose best clips were from The Daily Bruin back in the eighties? It may be the New Millennium but I know how the patriarchy works."

Brad lampooned pulling an imaginary arrow from his heart. "Present company excluded," I clarified.

"So you took matters into your own hands and started a blog."

"Right. And I did it assuming that no one would read my man-on-the- street interviews except the sources themselves. But surprisingly, within about six months, I had lots of daily hits, a steady stream of loyal readers who commented on my posts, and a teeny bit of advertising that covered gas and a new laptop."

"Then came the podcast...."

"Yes. A couple of months ago, before Alex went away to college in Austin, he convinced me to convert Peeps the blog into Peeps the podcast. I don't know why it hadn't occurred to me because I'd long lamented that too many podcasts were about only extraordinary people. You know, scoundrels, killers, inventors, geniuses. I'd been searching

for a podcast about everyday people but never found one. One of my college professors used to say, 'You can see the world in a grain of sand.'"

"Ah, the show's tag line!" "You really *have* listened."

"You doubted me?" he simulated another arrow through the heart. "I heard the one about the grandson of sharecroppers who spent years as a postal carrier. And the one about the movie-loving priest who ties every sermon to a film."

"So, yeah, that's the premise of Peeps: that everyone's life — even the smallest, most insular life — is a story worth hearing."

We were about to turn off the beach path and onto the city streets. We tossed our empty mocha cups into a blue recycling bin. He placed a hand on my lower back as we crossed Palisades Avenue, which made me feel dainty.

"Was it hard?" he said. "Starting a podcast?"

"If I didn't have Alex, yes. But he taught me how to use Garageband to record, how to find a hosting service, how to submit shows to distributors. He helped me pick out a mic. Later, I added a mic stand, a pop filter, and found a do-it-yourself graphic design app to change my logo from simply 'Peeps' to 'Peeps Podcast.'"

"You must be happy you did it."

We'd reached the Monterey cypress in front of his house. "I am."

"Do I detect a hint of hesitation?" Brad said.

Man, he was perceptive. "No," I said. "Well, maybe. I love doing the podcast. I just have this low-grade, nagging concern about keeping it sustainable."

"What do you mean? I thought the whole idea is that everyone's life is interesting. So unless you plan on making literally billions of episodes, you'll never run out of content."

"It's not that. Or not that exactly," I said. "With the blog posts, I interviewed people — people from all over the place — by phone. But a podcast requires sound and I've vowed to do all interviews in person. I don't want any over-the-phone hum. Even the most high-tech recording equipment can't mask that. And I want to be *with* the sources."

"Why does that matter?"

"I want listeners to hear for themselves the...nuances. The sadness behind an offhand laugh, the southerner's twang, the exhaustion of a new parent. I love the intimacy of the audio format, but I can't just keep interviewing people from Southern California. Listeners will get bored. I might too." A couple on a tandem bike jingled their bell as they rode past us. "So, anyway, that's a wrinkle I haven't sorted out yet."

Brad smiled at me but didn't comment on my conundrum. It didn't matter. I really just hoped that he'd invite me inside, the next milestone in our burgeoning relationship. Yes, my mother's memorial was that morning but I didn't want to think about it. I was ready for my second kiss.

But instead he said, "Well, I'm sure you're worn out from the day."

Had my mother's funeral really been just hours ago? He assumed, as most people would, that I was in mourning, exhausted from grief. But the truth was, I felt an enormous release, not just from the obligation of taking care of her in her final weeks. It was a release from my mother herself, one that I'd longed for as long as I could remember.

"Yeah," I said, hoping my disappointment in not being asked inside was interpreted as the grief I was expected to have.

"Let's talk soon." Brad hugged me, planting a kiss on the top of my head, and went inside.

I stood there on Adelaide Drive not wanting to go home but not knowing where to go instead. My friends would assume, like Brad had, that I was too sad to socialize. And I didn't want to intrude on Jeff and Milt.

Just then, a petite woman with blond hair that shimmered in the fading afternoon sunlight who may or may not have been Reese Witherspoon passed by me with an oversized orange purse slung glamorously over her shoulder. I remained still and watched her walk, her thick shiny hair swaying with each step.

I wanted to be someone with the need for such a bag. But I usually wore a fanny pack and I was not going for an ironic or retro look. I carried with me merely the essentials — hand sanitizer, my wallet, my phone — with no need for a big orange bag. Someone who carried a big orange purse like that had a Big Life. I don't mean big like chartering a private jet to Cabo on a moment's notice. No, to me, a Big Life meant living with a distinct joie de vivre, a conspicuous engagement with life, a desire to celebrate little things, which turned them into big things. A person with a bag like that had symphony tickets and dinner parties, a stack of hardcovers to read and knowledge of skin care.

If people won't have much to say about you at your funeral (as I observed that very morning), if YouTube thinks all you're interested in is "Secrets You Never Knew about the Cast of Friends," then you're not leading the kind of Big Life I'm talking about. People with Big Lives I know: the woman who threw a reveal party when she received her pet mutt's DNA results, complete with huge balloons spelling the dog's name, a guessing game and cake. And my neighbor who hosted free pop-up classes in her kitchen teaching how to make authentic pot stickers exactly like her grandmother taught her. And the man whose "Fridays with Mom" Instagram account cataloged the adventures he planned — "Tasting Afghan food for the first time," "Mom at a Beyoncé concert" — for his eighty-three-year-old mother.

I wanted to ask Big-Orange-Purse Reese what she was carrying in that bag. Then I wanted to ask about her life's pivot moment, one of my favorite Peeps questions. But she was already out of sight.

I remained still on the sidewalk, the setting sun beating onto my scalp, caught between longing for a Big Life and the momentum of how mine had simply unfolded. Mine certainly wasn't a bad life, but it wasn't a big one. And my longing was confusing — after all, with Peeps, I *celebrated* little lives.

Could I even have a Big Life? I shook the thought out of my head like a swimmer knocking water from her ear. Big Lives, for all of their allure, were scary, carrying risks like defeat or disappointment. Still, *foreclosing* the chance at a Big Life was as frightening to me as pursuing one.

Finally, with no other options, I crossed the street, got into my car and drove home.

Hi. Welcome to episode seventeen of Peeps, the podcast where you can find the world in a grain of sand.

The Oceanside Hill branch of the Ventura library is a sleek, recently remodeled mid-century building. It features glass-enclosed reading rooms, oak stairs and even a small cafe. There I met Marcus, a friend of Renee who was interviewed back in episode four, on a sunny afternoon where we sat in the courtyard with its view of horse property just beyond the library. The scent there was a mixture of hay and sea salt. A stout guy with a shaved head and an expansive smile that fills the entire bottom half of his face, Marcus looks like a high school football coach. But that's not what he does.

Marcus, seven billion people live on this earth. What's it like to be *you* right now?

I'm a librarian here in Ventura. After college, I spent eighteen crappy months selling industrial carpets. Thought I was going to lose it. Just lose it. Boring and pointless, that work. No offense to anyone who does it. Just wasn't for me. One day of particularly uninspired work, I asked myself what I really enjoyed doing. Where was I, you know, happy? When I really thought about it, library images popped into my mind. I still remember getting my first library card at a small library up north in San Mateo where I grew up. I was only about five but I remember it for sure. I love the smell of libraries. The near, but not total, silence. I was a jock in high school, didn't ever spend much time in the school library, but I loved it there too. Even someone with my large build could, you know, kind of hide among the tall stacks. Sometimes I'd tell my buddies I had to do research for a paper when actually I just wanted to *be* in the library.

Go on...

So, yeah. I got a wrestling scholarship to UC Berkeley. It has the most spectacular libraries. Most people studied in Doe. It was like right out of movie. Majestic like a church, picturesque like a centuries-old Ivy League college. It's got old-fashioned lamps in the reading room and

long tables where everyone flirted instead of studying. But as pretty as Doe was, I actually preferred "sleeper" libraries, as I thought of them. The one-room library in the paleontology building, the earth sciences library with its displays of rocks and old, dusty notebooks. Anyway, the point is, I loved libraries. Being in them. But also — and this is key — the philosophy behind them. The intellectual freedom and democracy of it all. So I ditched that awful carpet-selling job and went back to school. Got a master's in library and information science. I started off in an Oxnard middle school library. Then came here about, let's see, nine years ago now. It's a wonderful job. Mostly. In recent years, I've come to fear that I'm, um, going to be shot.

You— I'm sorry, *what*?

I'm chief librarian. Here almost every hour we're open. And I'm in charge. So I've gotta be the one to deescalate conflicts. Ask people to leave when necessary. A homeless person using the bathroom to bathe or sleep or shoot up. I mean, this magnificent institution is also a de facto shelter. My degree is in library science but I'm as much a social worker. A homeless woman actually died in the bathroom upstairs. Or it could be two teenagers who get into it about...whatever. Or it could be

the person who starts yelling because he knows he returned all the books he checked out and refuses to pay the seventy-five cent late fine. I've dealt with this kinda stuff and more. These days, librarians — of all people — are on the front lines of the opioid epidemic, of homelessness. I'm mostly okay with it. But as you saw when you came in, my desk is right by the front door. So the city requires me to attend active shooter training every year. It's utterly unnerving. I try to concentrate on what I love about being a librarian. Helping to preserve history, being a center of education. Recently, a teenager thanked me because for her, this is a place to go when she feels unsafe at home.

That does sound challenging. Marcus, tell me about your background.

Let's see.... Well, here's something: I was one of four kids growing up and I'm smack in the middle. Like really the middle because my two younger brothers are twins.

That sounds like a fun upbringing. And if you could take one physical object with you after you die, what would it be?

So my dad passed away a few years ago. I had the oh-so-fun job

of cleaning out his house. I found a box of his mother's — my grandmother's — belongings. More like mementos, right? I didn't know my grandmother. She died before I was born. It was mostly junk, as you might expect. But I did find an old journal. It was old, probably from the sixties. Spiral-bound. Pages crisp and yellowed. Inside was a list of books. Things like *In Cold Blood* and *Flowers for Algernon* and *The Wizard of Oz*. Better than that, it included the names of her friends who'd borrowed each book, the date she'd given it to them and whether it had been returned. Took me a minute to realize that she was her own personal librarian! Remarkable to me. No wonder I ended up in this job. So I'd take that.

What's one thing you do every day?

I've got an eleven-year-old daughter, Izzy, who lives most of the week with her mom. We're divorced. They live about two miles from my apartment. Every morning, I go on a run. Izzy's house is the half- way point, the spot I turn around. At precisely five minutes after seven, I knock on her window. I'm her alarm clock. It's a way for me to see her every day.

What was your pivot moment? In other words, what was the moment when something shifted for you?

Oh, easy. After my divorce — this was, let me see, about four years ago — I was at a New Year's Eve party. Afterwards, the host posted photos from the party online. I saw a picture of myself. I was like, I don't know, stunned. I mean, I'd seen the number on the scale. But I hadn't quite registered how heavy I'd gotten. I looked bloated. Like someone made one of those blow-up Halloween costumes of me. I looked downright awful. A switch was, like, you know, flipped. I stopped overeating. Immediately. Quit smoking cold turkey. I was down, really down, about my divorce. Being separated from Izzy. But I knew I wanted to live. It's probably why I'm so afraid of getting killed at work.

Who is someone you never saw again?

What do you mean?

I mean, is there someone in your life, someone important or someone fleeting, who you once knew or briefly crossed paths with, who you think about but no longer know or see?

Oh, yeah. Definitely. First person who comes to mind is a kid who moved into my neighborhood when I was in fourth grade. Same home room as me. He was different than me, though. I was big and not much into school back then. He was skinny and studious. But we, I don't know, clicked. His name was David. I don't remember anything about him other than he had blond, kind of frizzy hair, a lisp, and he told me that his mom had leukemia. Super nice kid. His backyard had this cool tree house. It was the bomb. We hung out there after school many afternoons that year. At school, we were in different friend groups. Matter of fact, some of the dopey guys I hung out with made fun of David's lisp behind his back. Hope he never knew that. Summer after fourth grade, his family moved away. I don't know where, when or why. Don't remember his last name. He was only in my school a year. Your question makes me realize I actually wonder about that kid all the time. Did his mom die from leukemia? Does he still lisp? What kind of life did he end up having? I wonder if he remembers our time in the tree house.

What's your life motto?

Oh, I don't have some grand philosophy or anything.

Do you have any, I don't know, mantras? Codes you live by?

Now that you mention it, something I say to Izzy every time I say goodbye is, "Remember who you are and whose you are." I want her to *think* about her identity. I don't want her to end up selling carpet by default because she hasn't considered what interests her, what's important to her. And I want Izzy to know that she's her father's daughter. Not like I own her or she's my possession or anything like that. Just that she's part of a family that loves her.

I'd like to thank Marcus for answering my questions. Have a suggestion for a future Peeps guest? Send me an email and let me know.

***

Visit ErinGordonAuthor.com to learn more about PEEPS and Erin Gordon's other novels.

Made in the USA
Las Vegas, NV
09 April 2024

88483598R00132